BAJA GRINGOS

Dorothea M. Eiler

Remember Earl (Tommy) Thompson + Dody whom you hosted in Berlin? This is her book.

Love
Mom & Dad

BRISTOL PUBLISHING ENTERPRISES
San Leandro, California

©1993 Bristol Publishing Enterprises, Inc., P.O. Box 1737, San Leandro, California 94577. World rights reserved. No part of this publication may be reproduced by any mechanical, photographic, or electronic process, or in the form of a phonographic recording, nor may it be stored in a retrieval system, transmitted, or otherwise copied for public or private use without prior written permission from the publisher.

Printed in the United States of America.

ISBN 1-55867-071-8
Library of Congress Catalog Card No. 92-075405

Cover design by Frank Paredes

CONTENTS

PREFACE	vii
1. WHAT'S THIS BOOK ABOUT, ANYWAY?	1
2. WHERE IN CALIFORNIA IS BAJA?	6
3. WHAT IS THE WEATHER REALLY LIKE IN BAJA?	15
4. HOW CAN YOU LIVE AMONG FOREIGNERS?	23
5. DO YOU SPEAK SPANISH?	33
6. DO YOU DRIVE IN MEXICO?	39
7. HOW DO YOU EVER MANAGE TO GET THROUGH TIJUANA?	48
8. WHAT IS BEYOND TIJUANA?	55
9. AREN'T MEXICAN LAWS A PROBLEM?	64
10. WHAT KINDS OF PERMITS DO YOU NEED TO LIVE IN BAJA?	72
11. AREN'T YOU AFRAID TO LIVE ALONE IN BAJA?	78
12. DO YOU HAVE ELECTRICITY AND OTHER CONVENIENCES?	85
13. DOES IT COST LESS TO LIVE IN BAJA?	93
14. DO YOU USE PESOS OR DOLLARS IN BAJA?	104

15. DO YOU DRINK THE WATER AND EAT THE FOOD DOWN THERE? 112
16. WHAT HAPPENS IF YOU GET SICK IN BAJA? 119
17. CAN GRINGOS OWN PROPERTY IN BAJA? 127
18. DOES ANYBODY IN HIS RIGHT MIND EVER TRY TO BUILD A HOUSE IN MEXICO? 135
19. WHAT IS THERE TO DO WITH YOUR TIME IN BAJA? 141
20. WHAT KIND OF CULTURAL OR ARTISTIC LIFE DOES BAJA OFFER? 147
21. WHAT KIND OF PEOPLE ARE THE BAJA GRINGOS? 152
22. WHICH OF ALL THOSE BEAUTIFUL SPOTS SHOULD I CHOOSE? 161
23. IS ROSARITO ONE'S HEAVEN ON EARTH? 171
24. OR IS ENSENADA THE PLACE TO CHOOSE? 180
25. IS THERE LIFE BEYOND ENSENADA? 187
CONCLUSION 194
INDEX 195

To Tommy

Without whose faith, support, and understanding this book would never have been written!

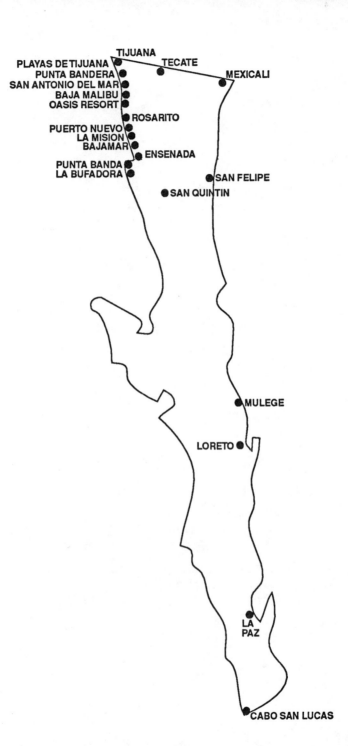

THE BAJA GRINGOS

PREFACE

We pour across the border in some 30,000,000 autos a year. Some of us come for a day to visit souvenir stands and to show a corner of a foreign land to visitors from far away. Some of us come for a weekend to enjoy the beaches and the outdoor activities. Some of us come to camp at the ocean or to relax at a luxury hotel. Some of us live here full or part time, usually in retirement. We are the Baja (pronounced Bah-Hah) Gringos, foreigners in this northwestern corner of Mexico, borrowing, for whatever the time of our stay, what we believe to be a piece of paradise from the citizens of another nation.

This specific piece of paradise is located on the northwestern coast of the Baja California (or Lower California) peninsula and stretches about 100 miles south of the Mexican border. I call it the *Azure Coast* because its dominant feature wherever you look is the blue Pacific Ocean. What is said about the area may or may not be true of other parts of Mexico, because northern Baja is much different in many ways than other parts of the country.

We who have migrated here from the U.S. often refer to ourselves as *Gringos*. The term is not easily defined, however. Sometimes it's uttered with a sneer, and Mexicans will not call you that to your face. But sometimes it is spoken with a touch of tenderness, because like the rest of humankind we are of many different kinds. Besides, it's hard to find a term for ourselves, as "Americans" is not politically correct these days. So we who are in Mexico, whether for a day or for a lifetime, speak of ourselves as Gringos. A female *gringo*, incidentally, in Spanish is a *gringa*, and you will find that I refer to myself as a Baja Gringa.

When I made the decision to move here, there were two things that happened that surprised me. First was the incredulity of my friends. Even now when I tell people in the U.S. that I live in Baja California, I find they are inclined to raise an eyebrow or tilt their heads in a way that implies serious doubts about my sanity. Then they often ask such strange questions that I am convinced that the old myths about the area have not yet disappeared. This book is intended to address these questions.

The second aspect of my decision that surprised me was that there was no printed material that I could find that gave detailed information about the advantages and problems that a citizen of the United States would face upon establishing residence in the area. There are plenty of guide books for tourists, and a couple of entertaining books about the experiences of those who built homes in Baja some years ago, but I could find no realistic description of what one is likely to face in contemporary Baja.

After I had made the move, I found myself frequently writing for the English language tourist publication in the area, *The Baja Times*, and it occurred to me that many of the articles I produced were really unconsciously written to answer the questions that I was constantly hearing about the area. I suspected that there might be readers who didn't see *The Baja Times* who would also like to consider the possibilities of part time or full time living in this border area (in Spanish, *frontera*) that in climate and scenery is like an uncrowded extension of Southern California. Some may want to really understand not only the many wonderful aspects of spending time in the area, but also some of the problems with which one will have to deal, even within the well-traveled tourist tracks.

One caveat that must be presented is that changes are taking place at a remarkable rate in Mexico, and especially in the border areas of Baja, and at the moment most of such changes are making life more comfortable for the Gringos. So as you read this book sometime in the future, be assured that it is unlikely that conditions will be worse. Most likely they will be better.

Great differences have taken place recently, and many former Gringos or others from north of the border who have not visited here recently may come to realize the differences that have occurred in this corner of Mexico in the past few years. Therefore another objective of this book is to make people more aware of the changes since their last visit here and to let them know what they can expect to see in the future.

So this little collection of essays is intended for those who are in northwestern Baja California, and for those who think they might like to join us some day in the future, either in fantasy or reality. The pieces herein have been fun to research and to write, and many people, both Mexican and U.S., are due my sincere thanks for their suggestions and information. This Baja Gringa also hopes that you will enjoy the book or at least parts of it and that it will lead you to increased enjoyment of your visits or of your life in our borrowed paradise!

Dorothea (Dody) M. Eiler
Rosarito Beach
Baja California Norte, Mexico

WHAT'S THIS BOOK ABOUT, ANYWAY?

It's about living in a very unique part of the world, a part of Mexico where most of the difficulties for foreigners don't apply or are ignored — a place where you can enjoy advantages of life in a foreign land without being deprived of most of the amenities of U.S. life.

Are you one of those people who is considering a different place to live, either full or part time? Perhaps you're searching for a vacation home and have heard of the growing economy in Mexico. Is there a chance to combine investment and a good vacation home? Or perhaps your work is in a home office, and you'd like to move to a more interesting or less hectic area. Or perhaps your company is offering you a chance to manage a twin plant or *maquiladora* in Tijuana or Ensenada.

Or you could be one of those people for whom retirement time is fast approaching. Maybe you've had a windfall and are thinking of early retirement. Maybe you've worked hard all your life, but are seeing those retirement figures as somewhat less than you had hoped. Will retirement mean a cut in your standard of living? Or maybe the figures are O.K., but the kind of lifestyle you want in your senior years is not available where you presently live. Is your present home area too crowded? Is the traffic getting you down? Or the crime? Or the weather? Is personal care impossible to get?

If any of these conditions apply to you, you have probably seen lots of suggestions about living in foreign countries as one possible solution. For example, in central Mexico and Central America one can live on Social Security reasonably comfortably. Or the isolation and ambience of island life may have an appeal for some.

But many people are reluctant to live in foreign surroundings and are loathe to distance themselves from family and friends. Flights to places like the interior of Mexico or to Costa Rica can be expensive and time-consuming if they have to be made with any frequency. And the retiree may find that young growing families often cannot take the time from careers or their children's activities to visit parents or grandparents at a distant location. Not only that, but trips back to the homeland can be increasingly difficult as the retiree ages.

Another disadvantage of foreign living is often the hassle required to establish or maintain residence in the chosen country. Special permits are required in some countries, even most of Mexico, and often the U.S. citizen must return to the U.S. every six months to renew his legal stay in the foreign country.

In many foreign lands it is also necessary to forgo some of the comforts that we Gringos take for granted such as telephones or frozen foods, or a variety of other products. Serious medical care may not be up to the standards we expect. We U.S citizens are used to our comforts and luxuries, and we may be reluctant to risk doing without if we exile ourselves in a foreign nation.

But we Baja Gringos have found a place with many of the advantages of foreign living but where we do not have to give up the comforts of the U.S. or hassle with foreign authorities. Because none of the above problems are present in the northwestern border areas of Mexico, there has become more and more interest in the area as a place to live, either in retirement or while doing home office type work, even as an executive of a manufacturing plant in the area. The Pacific Coast of the Baja California peninsula, with its benign year-round climate and its still uncrowded ambience, along with its growing economy, is attracting retirees, vacationers, and even employed people in the border areas of the two countries.

Most people want to have a pretty good idea of what they're in for before they commit themselves to such a move. We're all aware, I'm sure, that, though a realtor would never lie, it's possible that he or she might forget to tell us about a problem. Right? Ask a resident, and the answer you will get will be based on the experiences that the person had, maybe good, maybe bad. In fact almost anyone who answers your question will probably be biased in some way.

So this little volume is intended to "tell it as it is." The good and the difficult, the beauties and the "warts" are included here so the prospective occupant of the area will know pretty much what to expect. Be forewarned, however. The author is not a lawyer; so don't consider any of this as advice — though my colleague writer for *The Baja Times*, Peter R.J. Thompson, a lawyer knowledgeable about the laws of both countries, has been consulted on some parts of the book.

This Baja Gringa has spent five years living in Rosarito Beach, 17 miles south of Tijuana. Much of my time has been spent in research, and I have been active in the social scene, hearing the horror stories and the delights that other Baja Gringos have experienced. I have no ax to grind, though there's no question but that I am happy with the choice I made. But I'm not going to try to sell you on the idea of living here. After all, I don't want Baja to become a clone of Southern California. I'll just give you as many facts as possible. Then you may make up your own mind with some degree of knowledge about what to expect.

WHERE IN CALIFORNIA IS BAJA?

In which we clarify what we're talking about! That's not Baja, comma, California, but Baja (meaning in Spanish lower) California, and it is definitely not another suburb of Los Angeles, but rather a state of Mexico. Herewith a few words about its history and geography.

Once I wrote a letter to an editor of a magazine on the East Coast, inquiring about whether or not he was interested in a piece on Baja California. He answered saying he was sorry but that his publication dealt only with areas outside the United States.

I'm glad no Mexicans saw that letter, because Baja is consciously and pridefully a part of Mexico. But it is also an unique combination of two countries, a place where Latinos and Anglos meet on the Latinos' turf and where the Gringo adapts to Mexican ways even as the Mexican adopts many

Gringo ways. It's a place where the two cultures are less strained than they are north of the border and where they not so much clash as blend.

But this area is really new to the world in many ways, so I'm inclined to believe that when writing to anyone outside of the immediate Southwest, an explanation is needed.

One look at the map will explain why until very recently in history, this tag end of the world was almost unknown and was certainly unimportant. Baja California is a 1000-mile-long, narrow peninsula extending like the tail of a kite from the southern border of the United States and the State of California. It faces the Pacific Ocean on the west and the Sea of Cortez (the Gulf of California when I went to school) on the east. There is really only one decent even partly developed harbor on the Pacific Ocean side, more than halfway up the peninsula at Ensenada. And the narrow connection of Baja to mainland Mexico was a strip of truly forbidding desert until irrigation began there around 1920.

So geographically Baja was isolated. When Spain controlled the entire Southwest, caravans went from the interior of Mexico to Los Angeles and further north where the water was easier to find and where seaports were more accessible. But there were no precious metals or other resources to exploit in Baja; transportation was difficult or worse, and few expeditions turned south into Baja.

The Indians, of course, wandered throughout

the area. The Spaniards, who were the first Europeans to become acquainted with them, described them as very primitive. After all, they did not engage visibly in agriculture and wore almost no clothing. The good padres of the Church deplored such nakedness, but we have no record of what the soldiers thought, weighed down as they were in their leather jackets and metal helmets.

The Indians engaged in a simple and natural diet. There was no single food source such as the buffalo in the Great Plains or the salmon in the Northwest; so the early Baja citizens subsisted on a large variety of foods that they could gather or snare in simple ways. They ate grasses, fruits, cereals, fish and small animals such as hares or gophers, not to mention the very tastiest grubs, worms and insects. A real health food diet!

They wandered from seashore to mountains, and in the fall the acorn was an important part of their diet. Though there were certain sites where they preferred to stay, it is not possible to imply that they established towns or permanent settlements.

They did have a rich oral culture, and there are also some spectacular cave paintings off the beaten track in caves near the center of the peninsula. Not many people can get to them, but photographs prove they are well worth the extra effort for the archaeologist or hardy traveler.

So throughout most of its history the peninsula lay neglected except for some early rather pathetic

Jesuit and Dominican missions in the southern two-thirds of the peninsula. The northern third was served by missions farther north. In fact, it was with San Diego that the sparse population in the northern part of the peninsula had the most in common.

There were cattle ranches during the days of the Dons, and there were a few eager souls who attempted various kinds of industries in the nineteenth and early twentieth centuries, but nothing came of most of them. The various revolutions and governments in Mexico, the various cataclysmic events of the early 20th century, scarcely touched the almost empty hills.

In the second decade of the 1900s, however, things began to happen. The government of Mexico became stabilized after the Revolution of 1910, and the automobile became a viable means of transportation. The time coincided with the days of Prohibition in the United States, and the jet setters of the Jazz Age discovered that in their new autos they could wheel down to Tijuana and not only indulge in liquor but also in gambling and who knows what other activities. The gossip columnists didn't appear often in those parts.

By the early '30s there were bars and casinos, some very plush, to cater to the high rollers, and soon there was a decent road built down the coast as far as Ensenada, something less than 100 miles south of the border. On this blue coast which was fast turning to gold, things began happening in earnest! Agua Caliente spa, racetrack and casino became really world-famous, while the Rosarito Beach Hotel and the casino at Ensenada, late starters, nevertheless had their shares of glory and visits from famous people. Alas! the glory days were all too short!

First came the depression in the U.S., then the repeal of Prohibition. Gambling was outlawed in Mexico, and laws were passed against foreign ownership of property within 50 kilometers of the coast and 100 kilometers of the border, thereby effectively eliminating almost all of Baja as a place where Americans could own a home or a business. Tijuana continued to attract curious shoppers and a few youngsters determined to sow some wild oats, but for many years most of the peninsula returned to its somnambulant isolation, visited beyond Tijuana only by a few hardy outdoor types.

By 1952 more and more Mexicans from the interior of the country were attracted to the border region, and Baja's population markedly increased. The peninsula was divided about halfway down at the 28th parallel, and the northern half emerged from territorial status to become Northern Baja California (*Baja California Norte*), a state in the United States of Mexico. In 1974 Southern Baja gained statehood (*Baja California Sur*).

But perhaps the event that was to have the greatest impact occurred in 1966 when the government completed Mexican Highway One, a four-lane, limited-access divided highway from the border to Ensenada. From there a two-lane paved road continued all the way down the peninsula to Cabo San Lucas. Since that time tourism has gradually grown in importance in the peninsula. Now modern jet travel has made the popular areas farther south, all the way to the land's end at Cabo, more accessible, not only for tourists but also for residents.

The Mexican government, especially under the presidency of Carlos Salinas de Gotari, is once again welcoming the Gringos as tourists and even as residents, and laws and customs are recognizing the influx as healthy and profitable for both nations. Baja Norte became historically important again in 1988, when it became the first State in Mexico's history to be governed by an opposition party. Subsequent elections have been rated honest by unbiased observers and have proved that the two-party system is alive and well in Baja Norte. The proposed free trade agreement is bound to accelerate the changes toward freedom of the economy.

Nobody really knows how many Gringos live in Baja, either full or part time. The American Consul in Tijuana estimates between 40,000 and 50,000, but no one has an accurate count. By far the greatest number of them live in the corridor that stretches along the Azure Coast from Tijuana to Ensenada, but there are American colonies throughout the peninsula.

There are two large cities on the peninsula,

though neither has a large population of Gringos. They are Tijuana, just south of San Diego, and Mexicali on the east. The latter is the capital of the State of Baja California Norte and is in the heart of a rich agricultural region that extends north into California's Imperial Valley. Both cities are among the four or five largest cities in Mexico.

The eastern coast of the peninsula is the less settled area, with desert coming right down to the sea. San Felipe, about 90 miles south of Mexicali, is a popular spot, especially for its fishing and its expansive beaches. The weather, however, is very hot in the summertime, though usually nice in the winter.

From there, there is no dependable road south, and though Gringos do settle in various places such as Bahia de Los Angeles, they are isolated. Mulege is probably the next sizeable Gringo colony to the south, but it is easier to get to on the Mexican Highway One which crosses the peninsula from west to east just north of there.

Loreto and La Paz are important Mexican cities, though not noted for their Gringo settlements, but Cabo San Lucas, at the very tip of the peninsula, is becoming ever more popular for tourists as well as for part time and full time residents. The *cabo* or cape is far enough south to be in the tropics, and its stark scenery and equable weather are great enticements. Space is still plentiful although development is moving very rapidly.

On the west coast of the peninsula, the Gringo settlements are confined pretty much to the first 200 miles south of the border. At about 500 miles the highway leaves the west coast, crosses the peninsula and continues on south on the eastern coast. The lower half of the west coast is known for the birthing of the California gray whales every winter as well as for its other rare and interesting marine life. The major Gringo colony south of Ensenada is in San Quintin, and most U.S. residents are clustered in the northern 70 miles.

Facilities for recreation vary considerably from place to place, also. For instance, because of water problems and the scarcity of luxury-loving tourists in the past, there has not been a plethora of golf courses developed in Baja. Now major developments promise courses in several crucial areas. You must keep in mind that in Mexico the periods between planning and realization of such projects is unpredictable. They will be there someday, and things are moving faster all the time, but if golf is your number one priority, it would be wise to make sure that a course is already near the place you want to stay. In the areas near the U.S., golfers cross the border for their games.

Throughout the peninsula there are plenty of opportunities for other outdoor activities. The best known perhaps is the fishing of all kinds from dropping a line into the surf to mastering a marlin! Other water and beach sports are also common, and it's a wonderful place for wheeled recreation of every description from off-roads activities to bicycling.

Outdoor life is no longer the only thing that is important to the Baja Gringos, and the peninsula offers a great variety of social and cultural life styles depending to some extent on the area chosen. Obviously, those who live in isolated areas will find a much different lifestyle than those who belong to a condo complex of 100 or so units.

The people with the greatest range of choices are those who are clustered in Ensenada and Rosarito Beach to the north. This area is within easy reach of the border and enjoys the moderate climate and beautiful scenery that has made southern California in the U.S. world famous for its lifestyle. By far the largest number of Baja Gringos are on this Azure Coast, and since it is such an unique place, it will be the focus of our attention in this volume.

Any citizen of the U.S. who is considering a part time or full time home in Baja should visit throughout the peninsula. The decision on location will rest on your mode of transportation to and from the U.S., how often you will want to make the trip, what kind of climate you prefer, what you intend to do with yourself while in Mexico, how much you want to spend for living expenses. Whatever your preference, whether it's swinging night life or quiet contemplation, you can find a place to please you somewhere on this unusual, out-of-the-mainstream peninsula.

WHAT IS THE WEATHER REALLY LIKE IN BAJA?

Well, maybe it isn't perfect. But it comes pretty close. Herewith we consider the concerns and pleasures you may experience from the temperate climate on the Azure Coast.

If you enjoy a marked change of seasons, shoveling snow, or dripping humidity in the summer, then Baja is not for you. Remember this is a semi-arid region, sometimes called a Mediterranean climate. The average rainfall is around ten inches a year, which means that the usually few rainy days each year are enjoyed by the residents as they watch the soil and plants gratefully soak up the water and as the buildup of dust is washed away. However, if such cloudy, stormy weather continues for more than three days, many of us Baja Gringos begin to feel abused and depressed. We expect the sun to shine!

Yet it is not fair to say we don't have seasons. There is many a Baja Gringo who will tell you that winter on the Azure Coast is the best time of year. Usually the sun shines as brightly as ever, and though the air may have a nip in it that one does not feel in the summertime, it is really never necessary to bundle up with mittens, ear muffs and the like even for walking on the beach on the coldest days.

Nonetheless, this Gringa needs a central heating system. There are some homes that have only fireplaces or wall heaters, and though that is certainly ample for weekends and more than is necessary for summer visits, there are cold mornings in winter when the overcast hangs on, and the temperature is slow to rise, when it is too cold to get up in the mornings without heat, and when the cold temperatures will hang on into midday. Comfort demands central heating for a least a few days every year.

The tides are sometimes higher in the winter, which only makes the beach even better for walking. Tide pools develop in unexpected places, and the stretch of firm sand is wider and more varied. The walker is bound to come in refreshed and pleased with the delights of the fresh air and the natural beauty of the sea!

In some years, by the end of winter the beach is considerably diminished, and those who are unfamiliar with the various changes in the seasons may feel that it is ruined. But those of us who have been around for a few years know well that the sand will return early in the spring. And, even though the beach has been diminished, it is never destroyed. After all, who needs so much wide beach in the wintertime?

Not only that, but the beach is less crowded in the wintertime, which is not to say empty. On most days there are always a few sunners on the sand, especially in front of the hotels, while many more laze on the chaise lounges in the protected areas around the pools. There are certainly fewer people playing in the surf, because we all know the Pacific can be downright chilly in the winter. That doesn't stop the surfers riding the waves with, or even without, wet suits. Actually, they prefer the higher winter surfs!

In the wintertime it is much simpler to get around town and to find parking places. We Gringos can shop at leisure and run errands easily and comfortably. There is less noise from motor bikes or from late-operating discos, and there are fewer strangers to clutter up our small community life. The person you meet on the sidewalk will often be someone you know. In fact, this is how community news passes, between friends standing in the warm sun on the sidewalk. Who needs a daily newspaper?

Of course, sometimes during the winter it rains. Then we Gringos turn philosophical. After all, we always need the rain; so usually we remind each other of how lucky we are to have it, and we bear it with relatively good nature at least for a few days. There are some areas, though they're becoming fewer every year, where some of us many find ourselves mudded in. More and more streets are being paved, and in some places that were nearly impassable in the recent past, rain makes no difference anymore.

When the rain stops, we are often blessed by a warm dry spell, known locally as a Santa Ana. The TV weather people explain it as high pressure over the area to the east of us which causes strong winds to blow from the desert to the coast. These winds from the east can be harsh, occasionally even vicious, and since they blow over mostly deserted dry hills, they usually carry quite a load of dust. That's not to say that they create dust storms. They just cause films to form on furniture, window sills, and other areas that have to be tended to. These winds blow against the roll of the surf and often cause hugh plumes to rise off the churning waters. It can sometimes be a spectacular sight.

They also bring the higher temperatures from the desert areas to our coastline, resulting in beautifully calm days in the high 70s and 80s on the thermometer. So we use more body lotions, and bask in the beautiful mid-winter weather! The nights are usually pretty cold by our standards when a Santa Ana is blowing. The temperature will drop into the low 40s when the sun is not shining.

Occasionally the tail end of a storm out of the Arctic blows down the coastline in the winter, and such storms can bring extremes of weather by our standards. Once in a great while, if the wind driven waves combine with extremely high tides, there can be damage along the shoreline. One Gringa friend says, "The third time the water came in my front door, I just pulled up the carpeting and put down tile." There are even leftover ruins of homes devastated when cliffs crumbled in spots on the coast. Such severe storms are very rare, and never do they approach hurricane proportions. Damage is usually restricted to an occasional home here or there, and loss of life really never happens.

But the temperature drops precipitously, and on some days the high temperature never reaches 65°. Maybe once or twice a year there will be the white color of frost on roofs if one rises early. It's exciting to be out on the beach when the huge waves boom against the shore. There is something that, under such circumstances, makes it possible to renew a sense of adventure against the elements even when maintaining the caution of distance from the danger.

Whales and dolphins are seen more often in the winter, and the birds that glide effortlessly over calm summer waters struggle against winds and spray and move much more strenuously over the white caps on the disturbed stormy sea.

Gradually, as the sun moves farther north in the

sky, we find ourselves opening windows in midday, as is usual throughout the year, but forgetting to close them at night. From sometime in May until sometime in September or October, we pull up a blanket before morning and close only the windows that have to be locked at night.

The temperature range moves up by ten degrees in the reports, but there is seldom a Santa Ana wind to report or an Arctic storm approaching. It is now summer, and, on most days, the warm sun combines with a gentle sea breeze for a natural air conditioning that no manufacturer has yet equaled. The surfers read the reports avidly seeking four-foot waves, which are less common in summer, and they become ecstatic when the remnants of a tropical hurricane pass high over us because the surf becomes bigger. Such disturbances to the east of us can also cause some humidity and temperatures in the mid-80s. This is our worst summer weather, especially when the sea breezes fail us also. The flags or windsocks hang limply, and out come the fans. Now we Gringos have some weather to talk about and to deplore; so for a few days, we all gripe happily until the breeze kicks up again!

Sometime in September, or more likely October, we find ourselves closing windows at night while watching TV. In the morning, a warm robe starts feeling good, and then comes that morning when the heater must be used. Alas, the summer is over. But most afternoons the sun will warm our houses through the wide windows overlooking our views, and the heater with its thermostat will go on only spasmodically for the next six months or so.

Generally speaking the weather reports are repetitious and very unexciting. "Low clouds and fog along the coast in the early morning hours and clearing by midday," with lows in the low 40s in the winter and highs in the mid-70s in the summer. Day after day that is the report. Reporting the weather is not exactly an exciting job here on the coastline of upper Baja and Southern California, U.S.

We have no hurricanes or tornadoes, no extreme temperatures, and certainly no snow or sleet. The smog from the cities farther north has not yet reached us, and that produced here is blown away by the prevailing breezes. Our fog and haze is still grey or white, not brown as it is farther north. Near the power-generating plant in Rosarito Beach, there is a problem with a fine black soot that mixes with the dusty sediments. The plant is supplied with oil that comes from the Isthmus of Mexico in lumbering tankers that anchor off the coast. There is talk of replacing the oil with natural gas from the U.S., which will eliminate that form of pollution.

Other forms of industrial pollution are fast coming under control. A toxic waste disposal plant south of Tijuana was forbidden to open after the residents of Las Playas area demonstrated against it, and so far, in the actual area of the coastline there are almost no *maquiladoras* or industrial plants.

The only natural disaster that is even remotely likely to happen in Baja is an earthquake. Baja has not been mapped with fault lines as has Southern California, but there is agreement that the area may someday suffer a major temblor. Damage would be extensive, without question, but the odds are such that most Gringos do not have it on their list of things to worry about.

There are those from other parts of the world who sometimes complain about the lack of seasons, and they certainly aren't as marked as they are where Christmas is white and summer is green. There are those who complain that they feel the cold more here in the winter than they did in Duluth or Denver. But that's usually because they don't use their lined greatcoats in Baja, and their furnaces do not run day and night, maintaining a comfortable temperature without variation. As soon as the "snow birds," as we Gringos call those who come here to flee harsh winters, learn to live with the climate, there are almost none who would trade it for anywhere else.

HOW CAN YOU LIVE AMONG FOREIGNERS?

Or does my questioner mean, "How can you live where you are a foreigner?" One is scarcely a "stranger in a strange land" on the Azure Coast. The blend of cultures here is really unique.

Yes, you can tell when you cross the border that you're no longer in the United States. Things just are not quite as neat, as determinedly spacious, as they are north of the border. But once you get into life in the area, you soon find that there are as many things the same in Baja Norte as there are things that are different. So many aspects of life here are combinations of Anglo and Latino cultures. We will look at many of them in more detail in future chapters. Here let us examine some of the customs that make life a little different than it would be north of the border.

Everybody talks about the warmth of Mexico,

and it's truly more than an advertising slogan. People notice the inherent warmth of the Mexican people almost immediately. Most have ready smiles and cheerful greetings for anyone who speaks to them, and if they deal with life somewhat differently than do the Gringos, there is a certain amount of comfort in moving to their rhythms of life.

First of all, let me make clear, the Mexican is not lazy! Even in many parts of the U.S. today, it is virtually only Mexicans who can be hired to do hard physical labor. In Mexico, where modern equipment is seldom available, the Mexican laborer works long hours, six days a week, at digging and sawing and mixing concrete. Sledge hammers, not jack hammers, are used to break concrete. Mexican cleaning women would never dream of refusing to do windows or virtually anything else that you ask of them. The unskilled Mexicans certainly are not above doing hard physical labor to support themselves and their families.

Yet there's something about their approach to their tasks that makes the hardest work seem routine. They do not grunt or puff, frequently wipe a brow, or show any signs of difficulty. There are, of course, no formal rest breaks except for lunch, and so there is no fuss about sitting down in the shade for an informal time out. Instead the worker may lean on the shovel almost nonchalantly for a few minutes once in a while.

There is no sign of hurry or urgency. Even the

busiest repairman never gives you the sense that he is behind time or that he must hurry through your job to get to another who is waiting for him. As you watch a workman at his task, you will often think he's really being leisurely, but the skilled worker gets the chore done in good time and will often stand to chat a few minutes about your health or your family. They march to a different drummer than do we Gringos, a drummer who produces a less hectic beat.

And this less hectic beat leads to a different sense of time. Punctuality is certainly not the obsession in Mexico that it is north of the border. We Gringos soon learn that 8 p.m. in the evening for a function means that the affair will really get under way about 10 p.m. The Gringos are seated at their tables at 8 p.m., and they find there is nothing to do except visit with each other.

Around 9 p.m., the Mexican guests begin to arrive, and about 10 p.m. the master of ceremonies may begin the action. In fact many of us say when invited by a Mexican friend to an event, "Is that Mexican time or Gringo time?" The friend will laugh with you and reply, "Mexican time," to let you know that "on time" is not the time on the invitation.

Learn to live with the fact that if your repairman says he will come by at 2 o'clock, you'd better be prepared to spend the afternoon waiting for him. No one expects him or his office to call you. Probably there's no telephone or office, anyway. If time is precious and puts pressures on you, then Mexico may not be the best place to settle down.

But after a reasonable wait with no appearance for your requested service, you may conclude that for some reason he will not return to work for you. Mexicans rarely say "no." They do not want to confront you; so be prepared that "Maybe" or "Tomorrow, *mañana*," may mean "I can't" or "I won't." That's not always true, but it can be. After the second or third try, give it up and find someone else.

Lunch times for the professionals are usually extended and come late in the day by our standards. One o'clock is an early lunch; 2 o'clock is more common, and two hours for lunch is standard, during which time the Mexican may go home. Therefore, one does not see the crush in restaurants in Tijuana where everyone is trying to grab a bite and get back to work. But after lunch, Mexican offices are often open until 7 or 8 p.m. No wonder they don't get to social functions until 9 or 10 p.m.! Their time frame is different, no question.

Another thing the Gringo usually notices is a degree of untidiness in the city and on the streets, and some conclude that Mexicans are dirty people. That simply is not true. Check with anyone who has ever hired a Mexican housemaid. Or check any hovel to find the dirt floor cleaner than we Gringos could ever imagine it could be!

But there are several reasons for this civic untidiness. One is that there is not enough rain to grow much in the way of grass and trees. That leaves bare dirt on which every piece of litter shows up plainly. In addition, water is in short supply. Until recently, Baja has never had a dependable source of water, and with a rapidly growing population, there is certainly little available to nourish ground cover or trees, virtually none to hose down streets or sidewalks. New technologies and major efforts of conservation and recycling of water are making changes in this area, but the problem will not be solved overnight.

Another reason for the general untidiness is that there is not enough money to keep the garbage trucks, for instance, on schedule, to enforce leash laws for animals, to build a house from foundation to roof all in one procedure, etc. Therefore, one sees bags of trash that have been broken into by animals, houses that are half built with scrap lumber lying around, and other things that clutter the streets.

Those of us who have been around a while notice that such things are getting better. It seems as if the half-finished house does get completed and turns out to be very attractive. It appears to us who know the area that trash is under better control and that streets are swept more often, sometimes even with real street sweeping equipment replacing the shovels and wheelbarrows that until recently were the only method of street cleaning. Prosperity will surely accelerate improvements in this area.

A difference that Gringos often remark about is what seems to most of us an unusual number of holidays, and the Mexicans make much of them. There are several Independence Days, since the Mexicans had to make several runs at governing themselves. That means many parades each year in which school children take part, whole classes marching down the street with their teachers. We *Norte Americano* women notice that the teachers almost invariably wear nice dresses and high heeled shoes for the occasion. No self-respecting Mexican teacher would be caught dead in jeans and tennies when acting in her professional capacity! And the children, if not in historical costumes, are in school uniforms. Not a Bart Simpson haircut among them!

The *quinze* or fifteenth birthday party of the Mexican girl is great affair, starting in the church and ending up with huge receptions, attended by the friends of the honored, and also by friends of the parents and relatives. The major affairs are reported in the Mexican papers with more notice than is given to most weddings.

The Day of the Dead, November 1, All Saints' Day, is an important family holiday that is sometimes hard for the Gringo to understand. It is not a joke as Halloween is north of the border, but is marked by such things as picnics in cemeteries and fiestas where skeletons are part of the decor. In Mexican culture there is a different approach to death, one that Gringos have difficulty understanding.

Nevertheless, on Halloween the Mexican children in this part of the country have caught onto "trick or treat," and they swarm over neighborhoods on both sides of the border, picking up their share of goodies. Children in Mexico are usually accompanied by their parents. In the tourist areas and Gringo residential areas, others are kept out by the security guards.

The Mexicans are very proud of their families, and one seldom hears a noisy or unruly child in the supermarket. Nor have I ever seen a mother jerk one around. Even among the Mexican women who practice birth control, there is a certain joy, maybe even pride, in the accidental child.

The importance of the family affects things like human rights and feminism. There is much talk in the Mexican media on these subjects, but the results are rather mixed. In the case of feminism, most women who have enough means to afford some leisure are more interested in social life than in professional or cultural life outside the home. But there is a growing number of Mexican professional and business women, and even the less educated, younger women are finding their manual dexterity and willingness to work in great demand in manufacturing plants that are growing up along the border. What effect that will have on their future is anyone's guess.

In regard to human rights again, the stress is on collective human rights, rather than those of an individual. Without a presumption of innocence, criminal justice is not likely to be the long, drawn-out, controversial procedure that it is in the U.S. But the rights of the unions, of the *ejidos* (land owned by collectives) and even of the illegal immigrants into the U.S., not as individuals but as a group, are the concern of most advocates of human rights.

I once had a Mexican tell me, with a sense of pride, that the United States had the wrong approach. "In Mexico, when we catch a thief, the police have ways of making him tell what he did with the stolen stuff. And if I happened to have bought it, they would come into my house and take it away from me." The thought is really almost incomprehensible to the average Gringo, implying illegal methods and a complete disregard of individual criminal rights. *But* we do have to admit that such an approach must make it more difficult to fence stolen property.

A word or two should be said here about politics since Baja California *frontera*, as previously mentioned, has the distinction of being the first state in Mexico since the 1910 revolution where an opposition government has been allowed to take power in what has been, until the last very few years, a nation of one party government. Five years ago, the PAN (National Action Party) won the election for governor of the state and for mayors of three of the four major cities in the state. Elections had been consistently won until that time by the PRI (Revolutionary Institutional Party), and the competition between them is now serious and important to the Mexicans of the State. PAN recommends free market policies; so it is even possible to conclude that the Baja California Mexicans saw the light on economic freedom even before the Soviet Union collapsed.

Election day is a holiday, and no liquor may be sold anywhere on that day and the one previous. This writer was even refused a "Virgin Mary" as the bar did not want to serve anything that even looked like a drink!

It has become a Mexican tradition apparently for the losing party to claim fraud against the winners; so sometimes crowds gather outside vote counting headquarters and shout a lot, especially when TV cameras appear. They create a nuisance for the driver who hopes to get around that part of the city, but violence is not expected. Besides it's the army with big, scary rifles that are there to keep the peace.

It is not easy for this Baja Gringa to really understand what is happening in Mexican politics since I am unable to grasp the nuances in the newspapers or to understand the subtleties of Mexican television, but among my Mexican friends I find a new optimism, a belief that things are improving very swiftly in most areas. They seem to adore President Salinas, even if they don't belong to the PRI, and among PRI supporters, I often hear a grudging acknowledgement that PAN is making a real improvement in the government of the State. Nobody claims Mexico has ideal government, but almost everyone agrees that great improvements are taking place!

Actually, being a "foreigner" in Mexico has all the spice of a different culture without uncomfortable reactions. We enjoy the differences, and we respect their patterns and their pride in their emerging nation. In future chapters we will consider the myriad ways in which we are the same. In Mexico, because of the essential warmth of the people, it isn't at all difficult to live with the cultural differences, especially for a Gringo who wants to understand.

DO YOU SPEAK SPANISH?

The answer to that question is poco, muy poco (little, very little). There are some problems with the language, but they are not what you'd expect.

It has always been a conviction of mine that if I ever lived in a foreign country I would learn to speak the native language. As a guest of the people, that would be the only polite way to go. Right? Right!

So when I decided to live in Baja California, I made up my mind that I would learn to speak Spanish. Not only that, but when buzzing around the area, I occasionally found it convenient to use Spanish, and even on rare occasions a necessity.

Besides, I knew it was possible. I knew lots of people who were not any closer to being a genius than I was who could speak two or more languages.

Therefore, I tackled the problem with confidence and enthusiasm and made up my mind to be bilingual or to die trying. Well, the verdict isn't in yet, but if I were placing money on the proposition, I would put it on the latter alternative.

To help you begin, there are those columns in the local English language press such as *Spanish, Drop by Drop* or *Little by Little*. They make it sound so easy. The problem is that when I am somewhere where I need the conversation, I do not have the publication with me, and the words and structure have left my mind apparently forever.

Next step is to take some Spanish lessons. One finds that the language is very comparable to English, not only in vocabulary, but also in structure. "A cinch," I thought. My teacher assured me that I must get out there and use the language, and my years of teaching English made me certain she was right; so off I go. Whee! Now I speak Spanish. Right? Wrong!

I can ask the question I want to ask, especially if I make certain I have the vocabulary in place before I enter the place of business or make the telephone call. "*Esta Sr. Gonzales ahi?*" (Is Senor Gonzales there?) Then comes the problem. Instead of a simple "*Si*" or "*No*," I get a flood of Spanish that to me could mean either that he was away from his desk or that he had absconded with the company assets and they never expected to see him again. I make a few attempts to clear up the issue, but I am still unable to determine whether I should call back or he will call me. *"Lo siento, no comprendo muy bien, mas despacio por favor."* (I'm sorry. I don't understand very well. More slowly please.) Forget it! I end up saying *"Por favor, en Ingles."* — and the feeling of relief when an English speaker comes on the line and I hear the familiar words that I understand is a thing of beauty and a joy forever.

One of my Baja Gringo friends put it very succinctly when he said, "Why ask the question if you don't understand the answer?" The logic of his thought is devastating. Then there are the times that I use my Spanish and get shot down. One day in a market in Plaza Rio, I was looking for vanilla for one of my Stateside friends who wanted the real thing. I walked up to the stock boy working on the shelves and said, *"Donde esta la vainilla?"* (Where is the vanilla?) Unfortunately instead of using the correct Spanish pronunciation for the last word, I used the English pronunciation *vanilla*. The nice young man said to me in perfect English, "I don't understand you." So I repeated my question in English, and he led me right to the shelf. Bang! The balloon of enthusiasm is punctured for another indefinite period!

Surely as long as I live I'll be marked with a Gringo accent, but I know that people with strange accents in English can be understood, and in the border regions of Mexico I have a sneaking suspicion that the Gringo accent is not as noticeable as it would be in other Spanish-speaking areas. For instance, I've discovered that *dollars* is pronounced the same here in both languages, no *dolares* as in some Spanish speaking areas. However, the difference between an accent and entirely changing the pronunciation of a word is downright dangerous!

Another approach worth trying is to watch Spanish language television. Daytimes, just as in the U.S., one gets a lot of soap operas, and as far as this viewer is concerned, they are useless from which to learn. Sometimes I can't tell whether the character is suffering or proffering devotion. The relationships between characters with whom you've never before been involved can be pretty confusing in your own language. In a foreign language, it's hopeless.

Best of all, I've found, are the commercials. Sometimes I know what is being said from having seen the same commercial in English. Pictures and words go together well, and often the phrase being shouted on the audio is written for one on the video. So I can say, *"Crest para ninos"*(Crest for children) and *"Zestsacional"* in both languages.

Oddly enough, I find political speeches strangely easy to comprehend, at least in part. I suspect that that's because politicians in any country talk about country (*pais*), liberty *(libertad)*, economic problems (*problemas economicas*), etc. And proposed solutions are so vague as to be incomprehensible in no matter which language they are presented!

Probably my next step will be to take some time to go to one of those immersion-type schools where no one speaks anything but Spanish for a whole week. There are two such schools in Ensenada, and someday soon, when I can spare a week out of my busy Gringo life, I intend to really dig in and learn Spanish.

Part of the problem is that most people in this part of Baja have made it a point to learn English. Emergency workers, police, ambulance drivers, etc. study the language as part of their jobs and can usually handle it well enough at least in their own fields. After all, the excuses we Gringos use for going through a stop sign are the same ones used by the Spanish speakers. The policeman knows what we're saying even if he doesn't perfectly understand us.

And most workmen speak enough English to enable reasonable communication; though there are times when I think they understand me, and I find out they didn't. Oops! I wanted the weeds pulled, not the whole garden dug up. Demonstration is often a valuable addition to a conversation! It really embarrasses me, however, when my TV repairman comes to my house. When I first met him, he spoke no more English than I did Spanish. Now he speaks English very competently, but my Spanish is still impossible! We now communicate in English. What does that say about my learning abilities?

So we Gringos do not have to speak Spanish to get along because so many people in Baja speak English, and we are hesitant to ask them to take their time and effort to help us with our Spanish. They are busy people, and their job is not to teach us their language.

How many years will it take me to learn to speak and to understand Spanish? If you want to make up a betting pool on it, I would recommend the higher numbers! But I don't intend to give up!

DO YOU DRIVE IN MEXICO?

People frequently ask me that question; so here are a few notes on getting around by auto, which is really not that scary.

Actually there are two kinds of people in regard to Baja California. There are those who love it, and there are those who never go there because they won't drive in Mexico. They are appalled that a little old gray haired Gringa would wheel around Mexico all by herself. Most of their fears are either outdated or were never true to start with, but that doesn't mean they should be ignored. As we've said in a previous chapter, the tourist industry in this northwestern corner of the country that adjoins the United States grew up around the use of the automobile and the development of roads. Public travel geared toward the tourist is improving with the new laws that have recently been put into effect, but for the present, it is still necessary to deal with the problems, imagined or real, of driving in Mexico.

First of all *RELAX!* Almost nothing you've heard is as bad as you've heard it is. For instance, most Tijuanians are really very good drivers. They drive as if they spent a lot of time on U.S. streets and roads, which many of them do, and the traffic flow is nothing, but nothing, like Mexico City! Their autos, of whatever vintage, represent a major investment which they wish to protect as much as you wish to protect yours. Besides, this little old lady tooling around the city and highways has found that they are invariably more polite than in the U.S.

For example, lane markings on some of the city streets are not as clear as drivers are used to north of the border, but few Mexican drivers insist on maintaining their place in a lane regardless of the needs of the cars around them. Many times I have been waved into a clogged traffic lane when I indicated the move was necessary, and in fact, this is a common sight in Tijuana. What's more, it is impossible to imagine that any TJ driver would resort to a vulgar hand sign, which is now becoming all too common on the northern side of the border. Oh, there are idiots behind the wheel in Mexico, just as in the U.S., but the overall traffic pattern is more relaxed even in gridlock.

Another aspect of the drive south of the border that dismays some drivers is the condition of the streets and roads. There was a time when there was one paved street in Tijuana and beyond it nothing but wagon tracks. But such has not been true for many years now. It would be almost impossible to get yourself lost and stuck in the sand in some obscure part of Tijuana. The entire core of the city is paved, and all the throughways to other parts of the state are paved and usually at least four lanes wide. As the city expands onto the hills surrounding the core of the city, the street improvements have not kept up, but those of us who see such areas frequently are often amazed to see dirt tracks turn into paved streets within a few months.

Maintenance is, however, another story. Especially in the spring after the winter rains, chuck holes are unfortunately too common, even on the high-speed boulevards. Only the toll roads seem to maintain their smooth pavings. On most roads, white sand shoveled into the holes helps some. The driver can more easily see the break in the pavement, and the sand seems to keep the holes from becoming real axle breakers. Street repair is not always prompt, unfortunately, but it takes place sooner than it has in the past, and by fall, after the long dry season, the roads are usually in fine condition.

Because tourism depends so much on the automobile in this area, no vehicle permits are needed to enter Baja, which accounts in some measure for the some 30,000,000 or more cars that enter Mexico each year at San Ysidro (the major area for traffic from San Diego). However, by law vehicle permits are needed for travel on the peninsula south of Ensenada and on the mainland of Mexico. In an effort to eliminate the transport of stolen cars to the interior of the country, the government recently instituted fees for such permits, rather steep fees. This created such an uproar among Mexican citizens, that at last report, the law had been withdrawn.

Some people are afraid to drive in Mexico because of the horror stories they have heard about Mexican laws and police. It's true that some things are different than they are in the U.S., but there's no threat to the responsible person who really wants to stay out of trouble. Traffic laws are about the only ones that affect the ordinary Gringo very much, and they are very much the same as in the U.S. Speed limits and distances are most often posted in kilometers, and the easiest way to handle that is to think two-thirds. That is, 110 km per hour translates to roughly 70 mph. In distance, 50 kilometers is a little less than 35 miles.

The stop signs say *ALTO* instead of *STOP*, but they are the familiar red octagons. One problem is that there is seldom a *STOP AHEAD* sign to warn you of their locations; so they are fairly easy to miss. Driving in Mexico does require perhaps more concentration at least until one becomes familiar with the route. If you don't happen to see one of those *ALTO* signs, and if the policeman sees that you missed it, here are a few things to remember.

First remember that Mexico operates under the Napoleonic Code of laws, under which the accused is guilty until proven innocent. This is really hard for U.S. tourists to handle, but it might help to realize that the presumption of innocence is common only in the English-speaking countries, and that the Napoleonic Code is more prevalent in the world than is the English system. It is the code of law in Mexico.

In Mexico they don't give a citation and expect you to return later for trial or posting of bond. No, under their laws the driver is guilty until he can prove himself innocent. So, with that assumption, you must pay the fine at once or go to jail until you prove your innocence. Since the wheels of justice in Mexico move inexorably slowly, believe me when I say that there is virtually no viable alternative to paying the fine.

The policeman lifts the Mexican driver's license until the fine is paid, but not a foreigner's. Therefore, the rule is that the foreign driver must follow the officer to the police station to pay the fine where he will receive a receipt and be sent on his way. Stories about the horrors of Mexican jails, the time such a trip will take, and often a misunderstanding of the officer's explanation in inadequate English, may lead the Gringo to offer the fine to the policeman in the hope of avoiding the delay. In the past, the policeman too often has accepted what, at least to the Gringo, certainly appeared to be a bribe. Well, do you think he took it down to the police station and turned it in as a fine from a Gringo tourist?

Police are better paid in Baja Norte than they used to be, and the state and city governments are trying to insist on strict honesty in the police department. Just as in the U.S., attempting to bribe an officer is a felony; so the best thing for the driver to do is just accept the trip to the police station to pay the fine. It's really simpler for everyone.

Besides, insisting on the trip to the police station will discourage the few extortioners that are still left on the police force. If a policeman refuses to take you there, he was probably after a bribe. The U.S. Counsel requests that such an incident be reported, along with some kind of identification of the officer, name or badge number, or police car number, and especially time of stop. If such things are reported to the U.S. Consul, the authorities in Baja are very willing to fire the officers that are guilty of such transgressions.

Just recently a new plan has been instituted as an experiment. The police now issue citations with an addressed envelope to be mailed with the fine to a post office box in San Ysidro, USA. As of this writing, there is no word on whether or not the experiment has been a success. If enough U.S. drivers pay their fines this way, both tourists and Tijuana police will be happier.

In the case of any accident, no matter how small,

the Napoleonic Code can create some problems for the Gringo. Remember, the assumption is that both parties are to blame for the accident, and both must prove themselves, right there on the spot, financially liable for damages to any property or persons, private or public, involved in the accident. Otherwise you will be held until you can prove financial responsibility or until the case is settled — in some decade in the future.

There is one document that proves your financial capabilities quickly and easily: a Mexican insurance policy. No matter what the terms of your U.S. insurance are, the Mexicans will not accept a U.S. policy, but they will honor a Mexican policy. Therefore, a Mexican insurance policy is worth its weight in gold for peace of mind, if nothing else, because we all know that accidents do happen!

All these facts are moot, however, if alcohol or drugs are involved in an accident. This is a very serious offense in Mexico, and regardless of insurance, the driver with alcohol on his breath could well end up in jail even when he should probably be in a hospital. No blood alcohol measurements here! Or he can find himself in a Mexican hospital and unable to leave it for U.S. care. Drinking and driving is the best way for a Gringo to get into serious trouble in Mexico. In this case, only the American Consul can have any effect!

The wise driver in Mexico makes sure he has Mexican insurance in his glove compartment and does not have any booze in his body. With those two caveats, driving in Mexico is like driving in any other city where you really need to pay attention to find your way to where you want to go.

For those few people who cannot become comfortable with driving in a foreign country and who, in spite of all my explanations, still believe I am somewhat out of my mind for getting behind the wheel in Mexico, I recommend the newly developing tourist-oriented public transportation, which is not the public transportation that the Mexicans use. Prejudices and language problems combine to make the city's public transportation impossible as an alternative for the fearsome Gringo, but there are now tourist facilities easily available to them that go to Tijuana and as far south as Rosarito and Ensenada.

From the Amtrak station in San Diego, there is a scheduled bus that will take the reluctant driver to a special station at the Jai Alai palace in the heart of Tijuana's shopping and tourist area. Or there is a shiny red bus that will meet him at the end of the trolley line from San Diego and deliver him to various places in Tijuana as well as to the Jai Alai Palacio. From there, tourist buses are available to Rosarito and Ensenada, covering the entire Azure Coast. All personnel on this system are friendly souls who speak fluent English, and the buses are clean and usually uncrowded. Of course, the reluctant driver can also get all the way to Ensenada on day trip tourist buses or on day trip cruises from San Diego, available at the various hotels or through travel agents.

So you see we Baja Gringos are not really brave souls when we go "cruising" around this part of Mexico. We are fairly watchful and attentive for such things as stop signs and elusive lane markings; we carry Mexican insurance, and we do not indulge in alcohol or other drugs. Basically these are rules that all drivers should obey wherever they are! Once we've covered the ground, we go our ways as comfortably as we would in the States.

HOW DO YOU EVER MANAGE TO GET THROUGH TIJUANA?

If you get off the freeways, you have to know where you are and where you want to go. Tijuana is a large city with a peculiar traffic problem; so here's some advice about getting around the city!

Some people have "bad vibes" about driving in Mexico because sometime they had trouble getting through Tijuana. No large city is easy to traverse, and Tijuana has about a million people and a unique layout that makes it seem more difficult than most. If you just wander across the border with no destination in mind, believe me, you can be in trouble. So here is some good advice from a Baja Gringa on how to navigate through the city.

It's so easy to get in. You come to the Mexican custom gates, and you are usually waved right through. Seldom is there a line except occasionally when the Tijuana residents are coming home from work in the U.S. Once when I faced a 20-minute delay, it was because the U.S. Customs were stopping cars before they entered Mexico. Otherwise it's so easy to get right in, and there you are in a freeway complex that could blow your mind!

Think of Tijuana shaped like an open fan, with the San Ysidro border crossing at the handle of that fan, and with the edges stretching out along the border fence east and west from San Ysidro. Thousands of cars per day are routed through the bottleneck at San Ysidro, and the chore of the traffic engineers is to guide the drivers as easily as possible out of the congested area and toward other parts of the city. Therefore, the first thing the tourist faces upon crossing the border is a maze of ramps, overpasses, and underpasses. Those viaducts require a lot of signs, and at least for U.S. tourists, the fact that they are in Spanish instead of English makes life even more confusing.

Yet, in Los Angeles or any other strange city, you would hardly take a freeway off-ramp if you did not know where it would take you, now would you? You don't want to do so in Tijuana either.

That's why the first word of advice is to know where you want to go before you get into the traffic maze, before you have to face those signs and make quick decisions. If you don't know before you cross the border, stop at the first tourist information booth on your right immediately after passing through Mexican customs, and find out where the various attractions can be reached. This is also a good time and place to purchase your Mexican insurance as recommended in the chapter on driving laws.

Here are a few quick words on some of the things you may want to do or experience in this unique city and a quick description of how to get to them.

Maybe you're here just to give Aunt Tillie a chance to say she's been to Mexico. If that's your purpose, you probably want to take the Centro off-ramp, which is the one farthest left as you cross the border. This route winds around under the other ramps to Avenida Revolucion, only a breath away from the handle of the fan. Here there are countless vendors' stalls for bargaining with the proprietors, some nice duty-free stores, where you do not bargain, restaurants of all kinds and classes, discos, and what the media refer to as "photo opportunities" with burros painted with black stripes.

It's best to wheel into the first parking lot or garage that you see when you get onto the city streets, because if you go beyond Avenida Revolucion, you've gone too far, and you'll end up in gridlock downtown traffic. But if you take advantage of those first parking opportunities, you will be able to walk to everything you or Aunt Tillie want to see.

Maybe you want to see another dimension of Tijuana. You want to see some of the art and culture of the city, some of the new architecture, or some of the fine shopping plazas that are frequented by the Mexicans themselves. Then you should take the Rio Tijuana exit which is the second lane from the right as you cross the border. This lane leads to the Paseo de los Heroes and other broad avenues, graceful with tree-planted center islands, and dotted by *gloriettas,* or traffic circles, with massive statues. It is from this ramp that you will find the Cultural Center with its Omnimax Theatre where you can see a beautiful dome-projected film on Mexico's culture every day at 2 p.m. in English. There is also a permanent display on Mexico's cultural diversity and rotating art shows of first quality.

There are some tourists who avoid the Rio area at all costs because of those *gloriettas* that can send many an unfamiliar driver into a state of hysteria on the first confrontation. We Baja Gringos find that they not only enhance the beauty of the city, they are also a very efficient way of moving traffic. The rule is to stop before entering and to give the traffic already moving in the circle the right of way. Once in the circle, it helps if you indicate with your signal light whether or not you are trying to exit on your right. Though not every-one uses signal lights, drivers look out for each other's objectives, and traffic does keep moving. When this Gringa first drove through Tijuana, there were signals at all these traffic circles, which usually resulted in total gridlock. Then the signals were removed, and it seemed the traffic moved much better. At this writing signals have been restored on the *glorietta* that carries the most traffic. So who knows what you will find when you get there? Personally, I like them better uncontrolled, but I'll accept whatever the traffic engineers think will work better. Besides, if things get really gridlocked, policemen move in to direct traffic.

Another advantage of the *gloriettas* is that they make giving directions very easy. "Turn right at the Indian chief," we say, "to get to the beaches." Or "Make a U-turn around the 'scissors' to get to the Cultural Center." At least no one has to look for street names. Once you get used to them, traffic circles are really not so bad!

When you come onto Paseo de los Heroes, think of the street as heading generally south (not strictly true, it's really southeast). For all practical purposes, west is usually to your right, and east is usually to your left. From this area you can head in those general directions to the beaches (west) or to the airport (east). Signs in this area also indicate how to get to the Caliente Racetrack, and one can sometimes see from here, between the new office buildings being built all around, the towers of the Fiesta Americana Hotel, which is right next to the racetrack area. It may not be simple, but then in what city are such directions simple?

If, when you cross the border, your intention is to get to the coast cities farther south with as few problems as possible, you will stay in the second lane from the right as if going to the Rio area, but you will follow the signs off to the left that say *Rosarito-Ensenada Cuota*. *Cuota* means toll road, and, following those signs, you can get through the traffic of Tijuana without a single stop sign or signal and you will find yourself on the way to Rosarito and Ensenada with really carefree driving. You will be traveling along the base of the fan, beside the border fence, in a generally westerly direction. The road continues west, after a short turn to the south, and heads definitely south after the off-ramp for *Las Playas*, the beaches. When you leave the border fence behind you, if you wish to avoid the toll booths, take the Tecate-Mexicali route instead of the continuing westerly route to Las Playas or Ensenada Cuota. Toward the southern outskirts of Tijuana, you will see another exit that says *Rosarito*, and taking that will take you through the hills to the beach about 17 miles south of Tijuana.

The shortest way to Rosarito and Ensenada is to take the Rio exit from the border, go through the first *glorietta*, known as "the scissors" because of the twin, blade-shaped towers, and watch for the large Ensenada sign. It appears at the second street to your right after the scissors *glorietta*. You will find yourself on a one-way street that leads to a four-lane road that carries you into Rosarito Beach. The only serious problem involved on this road is the rather frequent *ALTO* signs. Try not to miss them! But you will also be deprived of the beautiful drive down the coastline that you have on the *cuota*!

If you disdain all of these destinations, there is a very short route to a location that has appeal to some people. The far right lane after crossing the border will lead you into the custom zone of the city and also to the Plaza Amigo shopping complex. This newly developed area is visited by many, not only for its interesting stores and gracious ambience, but also for its sports betting establishment and for its famous restaurants and popular discos. There's also a supermarket there, and many visitors find it a handy place to accomplish the purposes of their Tijuana visit. In which case, the returning border lines begin almost in front of its entrance, and one does not need to get into any other traffic at all.

If your destination is the Tijuana airport, the University, the Otay Mesa border crossing, or the industrial parks east of the city, that almost all-purpose lane second from the right will lead you to the signs that say *Aeropuerto* or airport, which will lead you in a generally easterly direction along the other base of the fan toward Otay Mesa.

Tijuana really isn't such a difficult place in which to drive, but it is a major city with suburbs spread out on all sides, and you really should know where you want to go in order to be able to get there. Once you know your way around, even a little old gray-haired Gringa lady can drive there with aplomb. We Baja Gringos take it in stride!

WHAT IS BEYOND TIJUANA?

Spectacular coastline is filling with all kinds of developments. People are flocking to become part of the 70-mile strip from Tijuana to Ensenada, the Azure Coast.

It's as if someone had scattered seeds all along the coastline. What's springing up on all sides are new buildings, new developments, in various colors and styles, until the entire Azure Coast from Las Playas (the beaches) de Tijuana to Ensenada is beginning to look like a giant flower garden. Some of the blossoms grow tall into several stories; others stay close to the ground, but all turn their colors toward the ocean and bask in the sight of the lace-edged waves in the azure sea. There is no doubt that within not too many years there will be an unbroken border of stylish housing all along the coastline.

In order to see the Azure Coast, you must find your way through the freeway maze at the entrance to Tijuana. You hang in on that all purpose second lane toward the right, wind around to the left, following signs that say *Rosarito-Ensenada* and end up driving toward the beaches along the border fence.

This area has been a kind of city park for prospective illegal immigrants and their friends while they await dusk to begin playing dangerous, sometimes deadly games with the U.S. Border Patrol. As of this writing, a new fence, made of air strip matting, seems to have diminished the popularity of the area. There are still spots where people gather, usually where the ground dips down and where it is possible to see over the fence. There you will see a vendor, selling cold drinks or maybe warm sweaters, tacos, whatever. But the action has been considerably reduced in this area, it seems to this regular driver. Probably many have found another place to gather and cross.

At the top of one of the hills, the road swings suddenly away from the border. In fact there's a sign that says in Spanish and English *Dangerous Curve*. The road descends into a steep canyon and turns west again on the way to Las Playas (the beaches). The beach area is best known to *Norte Americanos* as a place for non-traditional medical treatments and for drug and alcohol abuse sanitariums. Its most distinctive sight is the enormous bull ring bordering the Pacific Ocean.

But this is a bedroom community for Tijuana. There are high-rise condos on the beach, and middle class townhouses going up throughout the area. It is primarily a middle class neighborhood although there are spectacular mansions, which cannot be seen from the highway, clinging to the cliffsides overlooking the ocean where the sandy beach ends. In Las Playas the bulk of the residents are either middle class or very wealthy Mexicans, though many Gringos are scattered among them.

Immediately after the exit for Las Playas, the traveler arrives at the first toll booth on the *cuota* or toll road. Like all other fees in these days, the toll varies with the value of the peso, but it is raised also from time to time. At this writing it is over $2 for which the driver gets some fifteen miles of driving pleasure. The toll receipt also provides rather extensive insurance coverage, much more extensive than just the liability insurance carried by prudent drivers in Mexico.

The speed limit is 110 km or about 70 miles an hour, and the road is easy to drive at that speed. It is excellently maintained, four lanes, divided, very limited access and with telephones every two kilometers that (hopefully) provide direct service to emergency bilingual help. It is patrolled, as are all tourist roads in Mexico, by a corps of "Green Angels," men in green trucks who help motorists with problems. They carry emergency supplies of gas and things necessary for minor repairs, and there is no charge for this service except for the parts or supplies they provide.

This toll road is famous for its spectacular scenery, and here in the northern stretches the Coronados Islands recline on the sea, with the rocky coastline and breaking surf in the foreground. Truly a beautiful drive!

In areas all along the drive one passes groups of homes, some of which are multi-storied and really spectacular as they descend the cliffs to the ocean below. Actually beach front is not common anywhere on the Azure Coast. Cliffs form most of the topography.

As a result, the traveler on the *cuota* sees only perhaps one story and a roof and remains unaware of the spacious beauty of many of those homes. The large ones on the hillsides on the other side of the road are more obviously recognized for their architecture and choice of sites. Not all of these, by any means, belong to Gringos. At least 50% are owned by the rising middle class of Mexicans.

Some seventeen miles south, you find yourself at the *delegation* or we might say subsidiary city of Rosarito Beach, which has one of the best beaches on the entire coastline. Rosarito is a part of the municipality of Tijuana, though it is hoping to become an independent city. The area is marked by extensive development on both sides of the highway, and it is certainly one of the most popular places on the coast for tourists to remain for awhile and for residents to settle. Even an unobservant driver on the toll road cannot miss Rosarito's skyline that is sprouting high-rises or the new houses and apartments on both sides of the *cuota*.

There are three exits to this popular community, and just after the third exit there is another toll booth, requiring another payment for an additional 50 miles of carefree driving. And be forewarned. At the end of that 50 miles, when exiting the *cuota* at the entrance to Ensenada, the motorist will have to pay again. To some of us Gringos, it seems expensive to pay the price asked for the use of the road, but Mexico, struggling with a huge national debt and many economic problems, has realized that it must be on a pay-as-you-go basis. Those of us who choose to use the road must pay our way. And the costs keep the traffic down, making the drive really carefree.

There is also an alternative to the *cuota*, the *libre* or free road. From Tijuana to Rosarito, it too is four lanes, mostly divided, but after Rosarito on south, it is two lanes and usually crowded. Plans are in the wind to widen and divide it, but it will no doubt be many years before such improvements are realized. It also winds up into the hills about halfway to Ensenada, and the driver misses some of the most spectacular coastline views offered on the *cuota*. However, for many miles south of Rosarito, the *libre* and the *cuota* run side by side, and the marked development along the coastline is visible to the *cuota* driver.

All along this stretch are condos, mobile home parks, hotels, restaurants, and many individual homesites. Literally thousands of Baja Gringos have found what they consider a piece of paradise here beside the sea, and this area can be said to be the heart of the Azure Coast.

Multi-million dollar developments are in process or planned. Entire communities, complete with golf courses, marinas, and shopping centers are being built, as well as countless condos, apartments and homes. You will see everything from earth movers just preparing land to recently topped out high rises, and For Sale (in Spanish *Se Vende*) signs are as numerous as the sea birds soaring above. Completed complexes are adding new phases as the early ones sell out.

Commercial developments are on the rise also. At the very least most store fronts in Rosarito Beach are getting new facades, and there are several shopping plazas developing, including the large new San Fernando project in the middle of the city which will be anchored by a Dorian's department store, Baja's counterpart of Bullocks or Broadway. There are some curio vendors along the *libre* who still operate from shacks, but many are upgrading every day.

New luxury hotels have opened recently in Rosarito, in Ensenada, and between the two cities all along the coast, and the dowager of Baja's first class hotels, the Rosarito Beach Hotel, has recently completed over 100 new rooms while upgrading its grounds, public areas, and other facilities. New luxury recreational vehicle campgrounds are opening from north of Rosarito to south of Ensenada. This is no longer the area for the hardy outdoor camper type of tourist. It is now a place where the luxury lover can indulge in comfort as well as in scenic beauty.

Developments tend to thin out about halfway to Ensenada, but that doesn't mean there aren't any. Bajamar, two-thirds of the way on the *cuota*, is one of the major planned developments. It already boasts a golf course, and it is to become an entire planned community including a marina and ranch-type homesites.

The *cuota* ends at Ensenada, but this booming city has broad streets, well marked to guide the tourist around and on to the sights beyond. The city itself is in the process of developing its harbor side facilities and shopping areas for tourists, and it has sizeable shipyards and other industries. Good hotels and world-renowned restaurants are available, and many U.S. citizens find part time or full time living here incomparable.

Ensenada is also becoming famous for its fine wines. The Guadalupe Valley, north and east of the city, boasts almost ideal conditions for vineyards, and several long established wineries have imported European experts or have trained their young sons in expert wine making. Wine tasting at Mexico's oldest winery, Santo Thomas, is well worth the experience.

Of course, Ensenada can be reached by tour buses from San Diego, and now there is a cruise ship that does a one-day trip down the coast and back. Some drivers like to go on to the Punta Banda or the point of land that marks the southern end of Ensenada Bay where there are some lovely beaches, new developments, and finally La Bufadora, one of the world's more spectacular blow holes. Details on the areas and the advantages and disadvantages of the various homesites will be covered in future chapters.

South of Ensenada the highway is only two lanes and not always as smooth as it should be. There is beautiful country as the various valleys come down to the seacoast. One of the best known in this area is San Quintin, a rich farming valley with the beauty and climate necessary to make it a favorite residential and tourist spot sometime in the future. There is a Gringo colony there now that probably numbers over 100.

Development is everywhere evident and is surely inevitable given the equable climate, magnificent views, and accessibility to the U.S. Ah, there will be those who bemoan the loss of the primitive beauty, of the endless brown hills and deserted beaches that they once knew in Baja. But like it or not, there is no way the rest of the world can be kept from sharing this beautiful peninsula. The jobs and economic gains for the Mexicans as well as the pleasure that will be provided for so many people, Mexicans, Gringos, and others, cannot be denied for the nostalgic delight of a few.

There were always some who loved the barren beauty of the area, but there are millions who will admire in years to come the colorful flower garden of development that is sprouting now along the cliffs and beaches.

AREN'T MEXICAN LAWS A PROBLEM?

What problem? Actually Mexican laws affect me very little. But there are some laws that affect some of us, and some U.S. laws affect us; so herewith a discussion of problems involved with laws.

In spite of former ideas about the border area of Mexico, it is necessary for the Gringo to recognize that Mexicans are a very family-oriented culture and frown on rowdy, unpleasant behavior in public. It is also important to realize that the Gringo is not in the U.S. of A. where he can sue for such things as false arrest or brutality. The Gringo cannot threaten Mexican law enforcement. Therefore, it behooves the Gringo to know the law.

For instance, the laws regarding alcohol in Mexico are in some ways more lenient that they are farther north; in other ways they are more stringent. We've already mentioned the strict election day liquor prohibitions. On the other hand, it is legal to consume alcohol at age eighteen in Mexico. It is not legal at *any* age to consume it on the street. Because of the early drinking age, there is more than one young Gringo who has had a bit too much on the first eighteen-year-old weekend and then staggers down the street sucking on a can of beer. When he is reprimanded, or even worse, arrested for the offense, it is not uncommon for him to become offensive and even, in extreme cases, end up in a Mexican jail, Heaven forbid!

Remember the Napoleonic Code? He's guilty. Period. Now, if there is someone who can contact the American Consul for him, he may get out by the time he sobers up; or he may not. Bad scene!

There are ways to avoid this problem. At all the tourist bureau offices there are announcements, either posted or printed on cards to be handed out, listing the most common crimes for which Gringos are arrested and the fines that must be paid for each. Gringos would be well advised to check this list before going out on the town and to abide by the laws of their host country. (There is virtually nothing that embarrasses this Baja Gringa as much as the Ugly American youth staggering down the street, making vulgar signs at any passerby who irritates him, and generally being totally obnoxious. And frankly, on holiday weekends we Gringos see far too many of them.)

That doesn't mean that all Mexican police are

out to get the Gringos. On the contrary, the list of infractions of Mexican laws and the fines required is only one effort on the part of the government to see that the officers in the tourist areas are fair and friendly with the visitors. Most want to welcome the Gringo visitor, but there are always a few who are out to take advantage of the stranger. To overcome such events, there is a special office, the State Attorney General's Office for the Protection of Tourism, staffed by bilingual attorneys and established to assist tourists when they have problems in Baja. Offices usually have prominent signs or can be found by inquiring at the local tourist offices, or even hotels or ordinary businesses.

Usually U.S. citizens who get into legal trouble in Mexico are doing something that would get them into trouble in their own country: reckless driving, drinking too much, being disorderly in public, etc. Legal rights are more limited in Mexico, and since Mexico is anything but a wealthy nation, even minimum comforts are not available in places of confinement.

If the worst happens there are certain things to keep in mind. When dealing with the Mexican bureaucracy at any level, it is important to remember the Mexican bureaucrat is not a servant of you, the U.S. taxpayer, as would be a *Norte Americano* bureaucrat, and therefore he is not subject to the U.S. citizen's desires as are the civil servants in your own country.

It is also important to keep in mind that, in spite of the fact that you may both be speaking English, misunderstandings can occur unless the Mexican is one of those who has spent a lot of time in the States and has become truly fluent. The language difficulty, plus the fact that the Mexicans show less sense of urgency than do we Gringos, can often cause much frustration in difficult situations for the Gringo who finds himself dealing with any facet of Mexican government. The best advice is to try to relax and be patient. Eventually it will work itself out, probably to the Gringo's satisfaction. But it doesn't hurt to have on hand the number of the U.S. Consulate!

Remember, too, that Mexican courts do not recognize or take jurisdiction over legal papers from north of the border unless the bearer goes through an almost impossibly complicated process of translation, certification and legalization by the Consulate. The wise Gringo, therefore, has a Mexican will to cover assets he possesses in Baja, especially those not covered by the *fideicomiso*.

For the most part, Mexican laws are little problem for us. Mexican income taxes really do not affect us unless we create an income in Mexico. The little bit of interest earned on a Mexican bank account, though taxes on it are withheld, does not require filing a tax return. Seat belts and motorcycle helmets are not required. We usually register our cars in California, so vehicle laws do not apply; and for those of us who still believe that smoking will not kill us tomorrow, there are no laws against it in Baja. In fact, there are some Baja Gringos who live here just for that reason.

Actually, probably the most onerous laws that most of us really have to deal with are those imposed by the U.S. on returning to that country. Surely the major gripe of all Gringos is the border crossing. Since San Ysidro is the busiest entry port in the entire world (even without counting the illegals), and since most entries are made by automobile, sometimes the greatest traffic jam in the whole world occurs at the border gates. Drug- and explosive-sniffing dogs patrol the lines. Custom agents look for fruit (that damned Mexican fruit fly is as serious a danger to the U.S. as is any explosive). The agents also look for more than one liter of liquor or more than one carton of cigarettes per adult, and for other merchandise valued over $400. And the immigration officers are looking for illegal immigrants trying to cross in the border lines like the rest of us. They've got to be kidding when the border fence is so easy to get past!

A sign at the border gate informs you that you must report to the customs agent if you are carrying more than $10,000 into or out of the country. In fact, I've been stopped by U.S. Customs as I entered Mexico to ask me if I were carrying $10,000 with me. Ha! But it did make me wonder. Turns out that it must be negotiable paper, such as cash or other negotiable securities. It is okay to write a check for any amount in Mexico if you want to buy a house, for instance. But I'm not exactly sure what constitutes negotiable securities; so once again, this writer cautions that you should ask the proper authorities about this if you have any doubts on the subject.

The inspector will probably ask your nationality, and U.S. or Canadian citizens are seldom, if ever, asked to show their passports. Nationals of other countries must show proper permits to enter the United States.

The border personnel are usually pleasant to deal with, especially if the Gringo declares his Mexican purchases. For instance, none of my Gringo friends who own pets have any difficulty transporting them back and forth across the border even though the laws can be pretty strict in this regard. Of course, the owners all carry documentation to prove the pets have proper immunizations, and most agree that once in a great while they may have to show such papers, but for the most part, they have no problems in that regard.

Now there are diamond lanes on weekdays for four (no, not two) or more in a car, and they are enforced on the Mexican side by Tijuana police. Don't get in these lanes unless you qualify (yes, kids count as persons) because down the way a piece you will be turned back to the end of the lines. Not only that, but you are subject to a heavy fine by the U.S.

authorities, currently about $250. If yourself there by mistake, you are in serious trouble. Trying to squeeze into the regular lines that close to the actual crossing gate is seriously frowned upon, and many will refuse to allow you in. Really, the fastest and easiest way to get across is to just get in line and wait your turn!

Also, even after you've made it to the border gate, you may be again delayed by the National Guard, who are employed only in the war against drugs. They are not charged with enforcing custom laws or immigration laws, just drug laws. For that you may have to face further delay if you are one of the unlucky returnees who is waved into the additional line. Ho-hum!

However, knowing when and where and how to cross can eliminate much of the hassle. We Gringos try to avoid Mexican holidays and Sundays, especially in the summer season. There are several conflicting theories on the best place to cross. Does driving across Tijuana to the Otay Mesa crossing on the east side of the city where the lines are usually shorter take more time than it saves? In the San Ysidro lines, there are those who insist that the farther to the right you can get, the faster you will get across, but others insist the shorter lines to the left mean swifter passage.

Most of us just get in a line, ignore the lines beside us, which of course always move faster, listen to the radio or read a magazine, and wait for our turn at the border gate. The greatest sin of all, usually committed by those who are not regulars in the border lines, is to try to change lanes. Of course, if a line suddenly ends for some reason, people resignedly merge one on one without difficulty. But usually the hassle of changing lanes will draw blasting horns and will end up saving no time at all.

We Baja Gringos have learned some of the Mexican patience. We always knew this was part of the deal, and we've found that if we just relax, it doesn't take that long. Sometimes luck is with us, and we get through in five minutes or so. In a real disaster, it can take an hour or more, but usually it's closer to 30 or 40 minutes, and we allow time for it. No need to hassle.

There is a new book which is available in the border area with explicit directions for what are hopefully the easiest ways to cross the border. However, in order to use it with any profit, the reader has to be familiar with Tijuana and its many streets. If you buy it, be prepared to explore the city!

So hey! Who's afraid of Mexican laws? They're really less problem overall than laws in the U.S. As long as we conduct ourselves decently we coast along for the most part without problems. Most of us can easily handle that!

WHAT KINDS OF PERMITS DO YOU NEED TO LIVE IN BAJA?

Permits? What permits? Well, yes there are some required, but few Gringos bother with them. There are some, however, who like to abide strictly by Mexican law, and some permits can actually provide advantages for the holder.

Actually, though permits are required for residents, it's pretty hard to tell who should have them. One of the conveniences of visiting or even living in this area is that it's possible to get along without either visa or tourist card. Mexican law allows citizens of the U.S. and Canada to cross into the northern 100 kilometers of Baja for up to 72 hours without written permission, but for trips into the interior of the country or for visits of longer duration a visa good for up to six months, without charge, has always been required. It's worth mentioning though that the office at Maneadero, south of Ensenada, where such papers for tourists have traditionally been checked for trips farther south, seems to have been closed. Nobody home there anymore.

In any case many of us pick up a tourist visa from time to time to make our longer stays legal, but mainly it is assumed that we Gringos each cross the border every 72 hours for shopping or appointments or something. Certainly none of us has been hassled about longer stays.

Every so often there is a new effort to enforce the law in Mexico requiring retirees who live here to obtain a year-long "renter's permit" (*visitante rentista*), known as an FM-3, and some of us have gone through the hassle to get one. It takes a few trips to the local Mexican immigration office, proof of at least $1000 a month income, passport or other proof of U.S. citizenship, mug shots, the recommendation of a Mexican citizen, and other goodies.

Apparently new regulations also require proof of a Mexican bank account. The Mexican Department of Exterior Relations in Tijuana must also affix its stamp to the U.S. passport, for which there is no charge. The photos and paperwork, which have to be done in Spanish, will cost about $15, and there is a fee of about $65, which is paid to the bank, not to the immigration official, thereby eliminating any charges of fraud. With such a permit we can travel anywhere in Mexico, and it legalizes our status, which might be important in certain obscure circumstances. It does seem to simplify some Mexican procedures in case of death.

It also seems to be important to establish residence in Mexico, which can be significant for some Gringos from Canada and the U.S. For instance, a resident of Mexico is exempt on U.S. income taxes for a significant amount of money earned in Mexico if that residence can be proved. And Canadian citizens who actually reside in Mexico are free to travel back and forth among the three countries if they can prove their residency in any one of the three. Here's another field in which the writer begs the affected Gringo to check with knowledgeable people if such provisions seem to apply to your status.

The FM-3 must be renewed each year, and, though no one is willing to commit himself, it would appear it will cost the same amount, or more, each year. Certainly this writer's first renewal cost that much. Much worse was the hassle the authorities gave me, sending me to the Mexican Consulate in San Diego to have my bank statement (of all things) translated. There are those who suggest this could have been avoided by offering the local officer a few dollars. Other Mexican friends insist it is better not to do so.

On the other hand, many of us have found that if we go to the Mexican Consul in San Diego, we can get a six-month tourist visa for Mexico for no charge. And many of us are proceeding in that way to make our status legal. Most of us, I think, ignore the whole thing. It's highly unlikely that it will really become a serious problem for any of us. The Mexican government would naturally like to get some revenue from us Baja Gringos, but nobody believes that they will make us feel unwelcome or deport us.

With or without either of the documents I have described, *Norte Americanos* are not allowed to hold jobs in Mexico. Some may be employed if there is no Mexican who can fill the position. For instance, you may see a few Gringos working in such fields as real estate or English language publishing, for which they must have a permanent resident's visa, the FM-2, which is somewhat more difficult to obtain. There are no Mexican laws regarding those who still have businesses or positions within the States and want to commute. Distances are not great, especially from areas around Tijuana, and there is a sizeable number of us who cross the border daily.

The FM-2, the resident visa, is also supposedly necessary for the resident who wishes to bring in furniture from the United States, but here in the border area, the enforcement of that law is pretty lax. Mexican international movers ply both sides of the border constantly, and major furniture stores north of the border would probably be facing bankruptcy if they could not service their customers in Tijuana and along the coast. Except for a short period when all the Mexican customs agents on the border were replaced by newly trained agents from Mexico City, Gringos' possessions have moved back and forth across the border with little or no problem.

Mexican government visas are also necessary for any Gringos who are investing in Mexican businesses and in franchises, taking advantage of the growing economy in this part of the nation. Personally, this writer would put her life savings into the first McDonald's in Rosarito Beach (maybe), but no one has invited me to do so. Financial advisors abound for those who may want to consider such a possibility but without doubt, a good lawyer who is fluent in both languages is the first essential for anyone who has that kind of thing in mind. Only such a qualified person can advise you as to which kind of resident permit you will need, as well as the more esoteric aspects involved. Surely opportunities are very inviting both to make a lot of money and to be bilked out of everything you have. Caution is obviously the word!

In addition to permits from the Mexican government, the American Consul in Tijuana would really be happier if we Gringos would register at that office though I'm afraid not many of us do so. The point is made that in case of disaster they would like to know approximately how many *Norte Americanos* to try to account for. They also often get requests to contact a U.S. citizen south of the border but do not know how to find the lost Yankee. Therefore they wish that not only the full time resident but also those who own a weekend place in the area would register with the Consulate, and they assure that the information is kept strictly confidential, unless specific permission is granted to give the information to certain people. If you don't want your ex-spouse to find you, the Consulate will let you know that she/he is trying to contact you, but will not give away your location. It also simplifies U.S. red tape in case of emergency or death.

This registration also requires filling out a form, but it's in English so you can do it yourself. It is available at the U.S. Consulate or sometimes at meetings of U.S. citizens where the Consul appears. It's certainly an easy undertaking and will expedite many problems for the resident.

All authorities in both countries emphasize that obtaining the documents I have described does not affect U.S. citizenship in any way; so some of us go through the procedures; some of us don't. No Gringos that any of us have ever heard of have been deported for being in the country illegally. That day may come, but it's hardly a concern that belongs very high up on anyone's worry list.

AREN'T YOU AFRAID TO LIVE ALONE IN BAJA?

Whatever can you mean? If you mean in regard to violence, it seems to this Gringa there's less to fear than there is in the States!

Sometimes when friends ask this question I think they're still imagining the Mexico of days gone by with a *bandito* riding up to my house on a spirited horse, wearing a bandoleer of bullets across his chest and a smoking revolver in hand. *REALLY!!* Such excitement should only happen to this little old gray-haired Gringa! Come on, let's move into the 21st century!

There are all kinds of people in the U.S. who still think of the Mexicans as lawless, but most of us Baja Gringos see no evidence of such dangers. This Gringa is inclined to believe that the really lawless Mexicans in Baja make their way across the border into the U.S. where they can easily find more affluent victims and a less oppressive justice system.

Not that life is free of fears in Mexico. Where is that so? Streets and roads require more care for safe driving because they are not built to protect me if I drink too much, use bad judgement regarding such hazards as speed, or if my eyesight is not what it should be. My home must be well locked up because there are many strangers in the area, both tourists and Mexicans from the interior of the country.

But I have found that most of the fears expressed by my U.S. friends are not valid. For instance, I know people who are afraid to come to visit me because they think their car is likely to be stolen. "Is it safe here?" they'll ask when they park behind my house. Those same people will leave their car on the street in front of their home in San Diego and think nothing of it. Yet car thefts and vandalism in Baja are less common than in the States. Mexico has made some very strict laws about auto registration in order to try to eliminate stolen cars from being registered anew in Mexico.

And others of my friends express fears of the police who some believe are "out to get" the Gringos in some way or other. If nothing else, these paranoid souls believe the police want to shake them down. There was a time when this situation may have been common, but, if so, it is no longer a valid fear. The Mexican police recognize the Gringo tourist or resident as good for the economy, and if exploitation occurs now it is the exception, not the rule.

Offer to go with the police officer to the police station to pay your fine. If he doesn't take you, you were very likely the potential victim of a shakedown. Such incidents should be immediately reported to the Tourist Bureau and/or the U.S. Consulate, with some positive identification of the officer. Currently all official authorities want to entirely eliminate such unfortunate occurrences, and the chronic offender does lose his position.

Sometimes a misunderstanding of the Mexican laws lead tourists to believe they have been shaken down when this is not entirely true. See the chapter on driving in Mexico for an understanding of the traffic laws in some detail.

Unfortunately, if the Gringo seriously breaks the law in such a way that he must be incarcerated, there is considerably less concern for his rights and comforts than he will find in a U.S. jail. Mexico does not provide very well for prisoners, and the Gringo who finds himself in serious trouble may well have some very unpleasant experiences. But in most cases, we Gringos do not see the police except to wave and smile.

There is perhaps more incentive to be certain that I adhere to laws and rules of the country because I know it is more difficult for me to demand rights in a country that is not my own. Yet I also believe that, as a law-abiding Baja Gringa, if a disaster overtakes me, there will be some real effort to see that I am not made a victim of undue inclemency unless I alienate myself by being totally disagreeable.

The fear of *mordida* or a shakedown from officials other than the police is also becoming less noticeable. For instance, there was a time when bringing almost anything in the way of building supplies, furniture, etc., into Mexico required a payment to a customs inspector at the border. It was an expense one figured into the price. Now, unless one is transporting a rather major item on which there is a legitimate customs tax, inspectors do not seem interested. Nobody who knows Mexico would be so foolhardy as to say that there is no *mordida* any-more. But it is certainly less obvious, at least for the Gringos.

In regard to fears of more serious crime, there's no question that burglaries and vandalism do occur in the Gringo *campos* or settlements, as well as in Mexican homes and businesses. Some of my Mexican friends attribute them to Mexicans who have been turned back at the border and who are seeking funds to get them back to their homes in the interior of the country or to pay the illegal guides, known as *coyotes*, to guide them across the border. However, many of the victims of such selective burglaries have noticed that the incidents frequently occur on weekends when there are many tourists in town, not all of whom are Mexicans.

On the other hand, there are in my particular area several victims of *La Loca*, which translates into "The Crazy Woman." She managed for some time to find houses that were not regularly occupied and to make herself comfortable in them for days at a time. She had a compulsive penchant for perfumes and colognes; so those were the first thing she used up. She raided freezers, camped on the living room floor instead of in the beds, never cleaned up the kitchen or bath, and sometimes left with small appliances that presumably she could sell or trade for something. Walking into this mess was traumatic for the homeowner upon return, but scarcely dangerous. She was a small and wily woman who was hard to catch, and when caught, her rights to freedom were considered as important as they would be in the United States. Furthermore, facilities to take care of such people are very scarce in Mexico. We have been assured that she has now been put into an institution where she will be cared for. Anyway, we hope so; though none of us are afraid of her as such.

Furthermore, I would trust my Mexican cleaning woman with my life savings lying out before her eyes. She would pick it up, dust under it, and stack it neatly in the same place. Never have I had a tool stolen or missed anything after a Mexican workman left. The only time I ever missed anything was once when I left the tool shed open for a weekend when I was out of town. Somebody took my skill saw, but who knows if the thief was a Mexican?

When it comes to the most serious crimes, rape and murder, most of us feel safer than we would in the U.S. When I was a single woman living in Southern California, I resisted living on the ground floor of an apartment house because, quite frankly, I had had an unpleasant experience. Second or preferably third story was much more comfortable for me.

But here in Baja I live without worry in my ground floor home in an area with only a minimum amount of security. Now that isn't because I believe that there are no bad Mexican people. It's just that I believe seriously bad things are less likely to happen to me down here than in the U.S.

The dangers I do face are actually less threatening here than farther north. Break-ins are not uncommon, but no Gringo has been the victim of a drive-by shooting. In fact, though I can't follow the Mexican news as much as I would like because of my limited Spanish, I have not heard of any such epidemics in Tijuana or environs.

As for rape or murder, I have never heard of one case of the former involving a Gringa, and only one Gringo murder, in which other Gringos seemed to be the major suspects. We women never hesitate to walk or drive after dark in the cities or on the highways of the area. No one more threatening or unpleasant than a curio vendor has ever approached me day or night on the street.

Driving through Tijuana at night, you will see many women out on the street alone, respectable housewives, carrying groceries or leading a child by the hand, or the legitimate working girl returning from her job. And one does not have to dodge panhandler types when attending an affair at the Cultural Center or in downtown Tijuana. If my car were to break down in the dark of night, I would have very little apprehension about a man who might stop to help me. Almost any decent Mexican man would do that for a lady in distress.

In fact, the most unpleasant encounters that we Gringos experience may well be with the "ugly American" tourists who visit the area with the attitude that in Mexico virtually anything goes. Under the influence of various substances from beer to who knows what, they are often loud and rude, sometimes vulgar and even dangerous, either behind the wheel or staggering down the street. In fact, we Gringos usually try to stay home or visit only in our own complexes or neighborhoods when the area is full of tourists from the north.

Something about the Mexican culture, whether it's chivalry, machismo, or a fear of the police system, makes the violent criminal choose targets that are less likely to cause major trouble. It's not that I believe all Mexicans are virtuous. They are just like all other people, but for whatever reasons, this Gringa and her friends feel safer for their lives in Mexico than in the U.S.

DO YOU HAVE ELECTRICITY AND OTHER CONVENIENCES?

People who ask this question really want to know just how primitive living conditions are in Northern Baja. The answer is "Just like the U.S. — well, almost!"

There are many places in Mexico where it is necessary to have generation of some kind to provide your own electricity, but the settled parts of Northwestern Baja are not among them. Virtually all the homes along the coastline have ample electric service. After all, one of the most striking aspects of the landscape in Rosarito Beach is a huge generating plant which, 'tis rumored, generates so much power that some is sold north of the border.

But the smart Baja Gringo keeps on hand a good supply of candles and in less populated areas kerosene lamps to use during inevitable power failures. Such accidents happen less frequently than in the past, and they are usually of short duration since the lines have become computerized. It's true that there are times when one gets a little provoked with having to reset the digital clocks!

Usually you will find expensive electronic equipment protected with rather large and expensive boxes that are supposed to save them from such disasters as power surges. For the most part, we become familiar with such terms as *spikes* and *surges*. The later is by far the more damaging and requires more than the usual power strip for protection.

Now of course, in the U.S. if such a disaster occurs on a line, the customers can expect in most cases to be recompensed for damaged equipment. In Mexico your claim will be cheerfully accepted, but payment never seems to materialize. Papers get lost, etc. Therefore computers and appliances such as expensive hi-fi systems are usually attached to a contraption, the operation of which is a mystery to most of us, but which we have been told is necessary. Just between us, although I have my doubts about its value, I haven't got the courage to do without it. Well, what do I know?

When people ask about electricity, they also are thinking about problems in regard to the other utilities, and none of us would pretend that there are not problems, though all agree that they are less than in the past. For instance water has been the bane of existence in Baja virtually since people first lived here. Most homes have some kind of water storage system; so if the water suddenly disappears out of the pipes, there will still be enough for the real emergencies of life.

Generally that storage is underground and is called a *pila*, known to most of us as a cistern. A pump is attached to get the water into the house, and as one strolls along a residential street, one is often startled as a pump starts up in the house one is passing. Some houses have tanks on the roof, or at ground level. For such appliances as a dishwasher where pressure is a necessity, pressure tanks and systems are also needed. If the water stays off for several days, water trucks magically begin to appear to fill the storage systems. Not all such trucks have pumps, however, so the higher level systems sometimes present a problem.

Even though it seems that the water shortage problem is much less serious than it used to be since new aqueducts have been installed underground, nevertheless when it comes to water conservation, we Baja Gringos have been experts for as long as we've lived here. Nothing makes one as conscious of the need to save as doing without that precious commodity for a few days in a row.

One utility that presents few problems is propane, the fuel that is used for heating and cooking. It is supplied in tanks of various sizes, the small ones like those attached to barbecue units in the States. Most Gringos have tanks about four feet high, holding 80 liters, and usually installed two in tandem. When one is empty, the other will provide the needed fuel until the propane truck can again be summoned. Some residents have 800 liter tanks, which have to be serviced only two or three times a year.

Don't let anyone tell you that efficient heating is not necessary in Baja Norte, at least not if you're a lover of comfort. Winter temperatures are frequently in the 40s at night, and most winters frost is in the air or on the ground once or twice in the year. Unless your home is tiny and cozy, some kind of decent heat is needed at night and in the early morning in the wintertime. There are even a few days when and if a winter storm blows through that your heater could run all day long!

And don't forget that virtual necessity for any Gringo, the telephone. There are still places, even in some urban areas, where they are unobtainable. When purchasing a condo, for instance, it is wise to check to see if the service is actually in place. Virtually all the new buildings are equipped with lines and jacks for phone service, but many of them are not connected to any lines that will produce dial tones or voices. And please remember that Mexican promises of dates for future service are never precise.

When installed, the Mexican phone service is often inclined to be subject to mysterious noises, disconnections, and other annoying "bugs," and repair service is not always easy to obtain. There are those who insist the best way to get needed repairs is to go down to the phone company's service yard early in the morning and persuade one of the repairmen to take his truck first thing to your house to do the needed work. How do you persuade him? Well, think of a way!

A word of warning if you obtain a telephone when you purchase a place. Do not try to change the listing. The process is interminable, expensive, and probably won't get changed anyway. Just keep the phone and pay the bill under the name of the previous owner.

Various communication services offered in the U.S. are available in Mexico — fax machine, computer modems, etc. From what I hear from those who have them, they too are not "bug free," but that is not to say they are hopeless. The Mexican system in Baja works for the most part fairly well and is getting better all the time, though what would happen if it were suddenly overburdened by something like a disaster is not pleasant to think about.

Communication by mail here in Baja is usually handled through the U.S. system. Courier services are available to get the contents of a post office box in San Ysidro or Chula Vista, and neighbors go back and forth to the States virtually every day. They are always happy to carry outgoing mail or pick up delivered mail for each other. Few of us have the courage to trust the Mexican mail system. Another necessity to the life of most comfort-loving Gringos is adequate television service. Of course, there is no public cable TV, though many of the new complexes have satellite dishes and cable service to the units or homesites. In most places on the coastline or on the hills immediately behind it, San Diego stations, and even some Los Angeles stations, are available with the usual antenna. Along with the Tijuana stations, broadcasting for the most part in Spanish, there are some dozen stations available without a dish or cable, depending on the weather and the distance down the coast from the U.S.

Many homes in the area have satellite dishes, which are much less expensive to install than in the States. The reception is reported to be excellent. However, in most controlled communities the dish antenna will not be allowed on your roof because it will obstruct someone's view. If such a contraption is among your plans, keep that problem in mind when choosing a place to live. Be sure there's a place for the unwieldy thing somewhere below the roof line.

One problem the utilities present the Gringo is quick and easy satisfaction in regard to billing disputes. Here is where the Gringo feels most his foreignness. If he is unable to speak Spanish, matters are even worse. Even for the ordinary Mexican, the advantages are on the side of the utility. For the Gringo, it is even more difficult. Not to say the whole thing is hopeless, but it will not usually be settled quickly and easily one way or another. Influential Spanish-speaking help is badly needed at a time like this.

We Gringos have great hope for improvements as the Mexican government sells out to private ownership. Without question infusions of capital into the utility systems will have a good influence on the infrastructure. Already it seems that the telephone system is being expanded and upgraded since its recent sale to an international consortium, and as service improves, perhaps relationships between customer and provider will also.

But it seems there is no hope for the gasoline supplies, as Mexico's oil industry is a politically sacred cow, once expropriated from the U.S., and now a symbol of national pride. Actually there are as many opinions of Mexican gasoline as there are Gringo drivers on the road. There are those who swear by it and buy it almost exclusively. There are those who would never let a drop of the stuff anywhere near their gas tanks, even the new unleaded, higher octane called *Magna sin*. For the driver who does not use the Mexican product, gas can be purchased just before crossing into Mexico, and within the 100 miles of the border, most can arrange to get back to the U.S. for the next purchase. Some even keep an extra five gallons of U.S. gas on hand. In emergency, however, there are always Pemex, the name for the Mexican gasoline company, stations within an easy drive, though at certain times there may be rather long lines.

So, to questions regarding the ordinary comforts

of life, the answer is that there are few creature comforts that we Baja Gringos do not enjoy. Sometimes they fail us, but we are never deprived of the beauties of nature or of the warmth of nearby friends. And those of us who have spent even a few years here see things becoming more dependable every year. As we all learn to say in Spanish, *"No problemas!"*

13

DOES IT COST LESS TO LIVE IN BAJA?

Once again the answer is "Yes" and "No." Herewith some counsel on expenses of life on the Azure Coast.

A lot of people have heard a good deal about how much less expensive it is to live in Mexico than in the U.S. But Baja is an unique corner of Mexico, and what holds true for other parts of that nation is not necessarily true in the border area.

Mexicans here on the *frontera* make many of their purchases in the U.S., and they see the U.S. lifestyle whenever they cross the border. Naturally they want to enjoy the same if at all possible. Most of them came from other parts of Mexico in the hopes of bettering themselves financially, and if they can't do so in Mexico, they can always get across the border, legally or illegally, and make a better wage. Therefore, they are no longer willing to work for very low wages. Nevertheless, it is still possible for us Gringos to live well in this corner of Baja for less than comparable comforts would cost in the States.

One thing that is usually less expensive is unskilled labor. Housecleaners and handymen still work for under $20 a day (but not much under). Rare is the Gringo household without a woman to help with the cleaning chores and a handyman to do such things as painting and at least the heavier gardening. This also means that home care for the elderly or physically disabled is often more practicable and affordable than in the U.S.

In fact many aspects of routine health care are much less expensive, even for those who have some kind of health coverage. For instance, Mexican dentists are very popular even with people who do not live in Baja. Many U.S. citizens go south for dental care. The offices are usually well equipped; the practitioners are well trained; hygienic standards are as high as any, and their prices are roughly one-third of those on the other side of the border.

Pharmaceuticals are another cost saver. Some over-the-counter drugs cost only ten percent of their price in the U.S., and all antibiotics are sold without prescription for roughly one-third of the prices north of the border. Narcotics, however, require the prescription of a Mexican doctor. There are some drugs available in Mexico that have not yet been approved for use in the United States. The pharmaceuticals purchased in Mexico may be taken back to the U.S. if they are for your personal use and you have a prescription from your doctor. See the chapter on health care for information on the costs of more serious health problems.

When the Gringo moves into the skilled labor field, the cost of labor naturally increases. Good electricians, carpenters, plumbers, and such expect about $40 to $50, not per hour, but per day. Good contractors who have first class reputations among the Gringos charge by the job. The work will come in at less than a comparable job in the States, but the Gringo who tries to get the cheapest work stands a chance of getting inferior work.

The Mexican worker is sometimes accused of doing work that is not up to standard, but the truth is, he is ingenious at making do with less than the best. When expected to work cheaply, he can do it, mainly because he knows how to "get by." For instance, when a plumber was repairing plumbing under the house he found a place where the pieces of pipe had not quite come together and a piece of auto heater hose had been clamped into the gap. Ingenious. Inexpensive. And who knows for how many years it had been working fairly well? It's true here as well as anywhere else that you get what you pay for — if you watch carefully! There are no government inspections of such work, but then there are no bribes to pay. Let the homeowner beware.

The most obvious saving is in the price of acquiring a home in the first place, though things are changing rapidly on the up side. By the time you read this, you may have to add to the following figures, but it will probably be only a small percentage for the foreseeable future. Nice condos, right on the beach, are getting close to a $100,000 minimum. That is nearly double the price of four years ago. A large penthouse on the top of a new high-rise will cost around $200,000, roughly one-tenth the cost for similar facilities in Southern California. View homesites in new luxury developments can be acquired for $30,000 to $40,000, with building costs about $35 to $40 per square foot. And such developments offer most amenities, such as full security, recreation facilities, covered parking, private water sources, etc.

Spacious homes with spectacular views, even right on the ocean's edge, may cost in extreme cases as much as $500,000, and there are even a couple rumored to be in the $2 million range, but when mentioned, their luxuries are always said to be truly spectacular. Of course, once more, in comparison to such properties in Southern California, the prices are far less than half.

Small homes, perhaps with ocean view, a block or so from the water, are still a bargain at under $100,000, and there are some "fixer-uppers" that can be acquired for under $50,000.

Another less expensive alternate is a mobile home. Parks right on the ocean, unlike on the U.S.

side, are fairly common, and lot rents run sometimes as high as $300-$400 a month. Some offer revocable *fideicomisos* (see chapter on property rights) for up to 30 years, but in any case Mexican law limits rent increases to 10% per year. Travel trailers on rented property in some areas can sometimes be purchased for under $25,000, but large mobile homes on rented lots in good locations start at about $40,000. Sometimes, when located on the beach, or when bricked or plastered, with additional rooms added on, and with a paid-up *fideicomiso*, they can run $100,000 or more.

Location also affects the price as it does anywhere else. There are many lovely homes in isolated places with inadequate access roads. And there are some in lovely complexes that are far from activity centers and from such amenities as grocery stores or service providers. It is also wise to avoid a place too close to the discos on the beach that are popular with the noisy, youngish crowd.

Another living cost that is usually less than in the U.S. is insurance. Homeowners' insurance is available in Mexico at a nominal fee. For one thing Mexicans are not as litigious as are people in the U.S., and smaller amounts will cover the necessary liability needs. As far as damage claims are concerned, this Gringa has found payment for claims of wind or water damage to my home have been hassle-free, although, like so many other things in Mexico, not necessarily prompt.

The laws regarding liability in automobile accidents are discussed in the chapter on driving in Mexico, and, since Mexican insurance is so important to us, many of us Gringos carry all our automobile insurance in Mexico. Comprehensive and collision, as well as liability, can be covered in Mexico for about half of the costs for similar coverage in California. And our Mexican insurance agent also can provide liability insurance as required by California law. At present such coverage represents a great saving over purchase of insurance in California alone, not to mention the additional coverage needed in Mexico. Not only that, the insurance agents know their Gringo customers personally, and there is a relationship that used to be common in the smaller communities of the U.S., that has disappeared almost everywhere up there.

Few, if any, of us register our cars in Mexico. That process is very expensive and requires a Mexican driver's license, for which one must be fluent in Spanish. Add to those problems putting in an application at a bureau with lines that go on forever, and you soon decide it's easier to maintain the U.S. plates.

When it comes to other car expenses, it is never easy to figure out how the price of gasoline compares to U.S. prices. You see, it is sold by the liter (about a quart), and by the time you figure liters to gallons and pesos to dollars, — well. However, among the mathematicians in the Gringo population, there seems to be some agreement that it is about the same price as in the States.

Almost all of us have car repairs done in Mexico because the prices are so reasonable. Jack Smith, that famous Gringo who writes for the L.A. Times, once said that "Mexicans love an ailing car," and we have all seen much evidence of the truth of his observation. Maybe that's why so many of them are really fine repairmen and body workers. Anyway, we Gringos have our favorites whom we trust absolutely. And even as the prices go up, they will still remain well under most places in the U.S.

We also certainly realize some saving on our utilities. Electricity is generally about half or less the rates in most places north of the border, and water is very inexpensive. Propane is also fairly reasonable, though it may be more expensive than natural gas is in some states of the U.S.

For those lucky Gringos who have phones, rates are almost exactly comparable with those north of the border, though the Mexican bill includes some 30% taxes. Many auxiliary services are available, but dependability is still questionable. Some of the residents outside of urban areas have cellular phones, and they are quite expensive, as they are almost anywhere. If phones are important to your way of life, and you are on limited income, better look for a place that already has a phone installed.

One of delights that used to be a real bargain in Baja is restaurant meals. I'm sorry to have to report that they are becoming more expensive with each passing day. Local chefs are being sent abroad for training, and restaurants are becoming more conscious of style and ambience. Yet really good dinners can be obtained if one knows where for less than $10 per person, and the famous lobster is still less than $20 anywhere except the most elite places.

Bar drinks run at prices of $1 for margaritas on special to $3.50 for call drinks. But one thing that is not cheap is wine for dinner. It is not uncommon to pay $12 for a bottle of local wine in the better places, and California wines are usually unavailable or even more expensive. If one glass is all you want, you will get it for about the price of a call drink, but it will not be a generous serving.

Another former bargain that is fast disappearing is for hotels and other accommodations. Prices are still good during the winter but, in the better places, are inching up as is the quality of the hostelries. Luxury hotels are rising all along the coastline and the sheer number of the rooms has kept the price beneath $100 a night — still. A new spa has been installed in the Rosarito Beach Hotel where prices, while still slightly under those stateside, are far from inexpensive. For example, in their beauty shop a shampoo and blow-dry costs $20. In contrast the various *esteticas* or beauty shops in the other parts of the cities charge $6 or $7 for such service. This is another good example of lower prices under some conditions that demonstrates how the Baja

Gringo can live better for less.

As for groceries and other commodities, most of us Gringos shop across the border in the U.S. Food prices in Baja are generally about the same or slightly higher than in the U.S., but the quality often does not come up to what we expect. Also, sometimes selections are limited. Maybe today there are no green onions in the supermarket, or tomorrow there may be no sugar. Stocks are improving all the time, however, as is quality.

There are certain things that we almost always buy in Mexico. Coffee is one of them, delicious and inexpensive. The liquor distilled in Mexico is also a good bargain. Vodka, gin, tequila and brandy are as good as the best anywhere and usually cost about half as much as they do north of the border. And don't forget that delicious Kahlua!

And it's an absolute sin for us to buy hard rolls anywhere else than in our neighborhood *panaderia* (bakery). They are so delicious and indecently cheap. Another heresy would be to buy tortillas anywhere else than the local *tortilleria* where they are presented to you so fresh they are still hot, unlike any packaged imitations.

Another aspect of our lives that proves inexpensive is that of our wardrobes. The standard dress is casual, tennis shoes, tee shirts, and for the women informal pants suits. Dress-up clothes are worn only for fancy evening occasions, Mexican receptions, or charity affairs, seldom to Gringo social functions.

Never have I seen one of my friends, male or female, in a business suit in Baja. I take that back. Saw two men in business suits in one of the productions of a little theater.

Not only that, but many of us buy our clothes from the little boutiques in our neighborhoods. Some Mexican designers and manufacturing companies are creating clothes that are not typically Mexican, but are stylish anywhere for roughly one-third less than the price of such clothes in the States. We soon get to know the people in the local stores and sometimes such acquaintances result in special orders for the customer. Reminds this Gringa of the old days in my small home town before the days of massively stocked department stores in huge shopping malls.

One advantage that many of us use is the duty-free stores just before we cross the border on our way home from trips to the U.S. The smokers among us buy cigarettes there at roughly half the going price in California, and saving taxes on liquor, appliances, jewelry, perfume and imported foods means many more such luxuries are available on limited incomes.

One other aspect that may or may not prove important to a Gringo who is a resident of Mexico is the tax advantages for money earned in that country. The executive of a *maquiladora* may find his salary taxed less and his exemption in the U.S. quite meaningful. Also other Mexican income enjoys a sizeable exemption, and the interested Gringo should certainly check with his or her tax expert in this regard.

Some of these advantages will probably always be true; some will be diminishing as time goes by. At present you can live better on a limited income in Baja than in Southern California, and to some measure that will probably always be true. But the two economies are too tightly integrated for us Gringos to avoid the consequences of being so near the dominant economy of the United States.

DO YOU USE PESOS OR DOLLARS IN BAJA?

Sometimes it's more convenient, even necessary, to use pesos, but usually dollars will do fine. A few words on dealing with Mexican money and the economy.

For the most part, money exchange presents no problems on the Azure Coast. Dollars and pesos are used almost interchangeably. The Gringo just says, "In dollars, please," or *"En dolares, por favor,"* if we are trying to practice our Spanish. The cashier then turns to a handy, dandy, little calculator beside the cash register, taps in the exchange rate, and in either Spanish or English tells you how many dollars are needed, usually showing the calculator display at the same time, just in case we cannot understand the amount in Spanish or accented English. The cashiers are skillful in making change in both currencies, and you will receive your change in dollars, not pesos.

Of course, there are those who will emphasize the fact that the exchange rate is not as good at the place of business as it is at the bank, and that is usually true to a small degree. The store may figure 3100 pesos to the dollar, while the bank is giving 3175. Most Gringos prefer to take the small discount to avoid the time standing in line at the bank to change dollars into pesos. Like other lines in Mexico, bank lines can often be interminable!

At the time of writing the Mexican peso was valued at 3100 to the dollar, but by the time you read this, it is expected to be about 3.1 to the dollar. That's because by decree the Mexican government is dropping three decimal places off the peso. In fact, it may become 3.2 or 3.3 or more to the dollar as time passes, but devaluation has become very slow moving in the past few years — one of the good signs for the Mexican economy.

Really, it doesn't matter to those who are purchasing things in Mexico how many zeros are on the end of the peso, but it certainly does make life a little easier for those of us who are not quite mathematical geniuses to be able to divide by three without having to move the decimal places. It was always such a pleasure for me to be able to speak with authority when asked in a grocery store, for instance, by an obvious tourist Gringo, "How much is this in dollars?"

I used to say, "Divide by three. Move the decimal

place three places to the left and knock off one percent." But I learned that those looks of absolute awe that I received were totally undeserved, and I began to feel guilty. After all, this little old Baja Gringa is anything but a mathematical genius. My sense of humility demanded that I make my answers simple. I could, however, look at a price tag reading 12,300 pesos and say with aplomb, "Almost exactly $4." Now I can just say, "Divide by three, and it will be a few cents less."

Obviously the reason for the change was not to put down us phoney mathematicians, but to make life easier for all accountants in Mexico. For instance, think how much easier it is to put things into computer columns without all those extra figures! Think how much easier it is for financial people all over the world to think in pesos!

Nevertheless, this Baja Gringa is disappointed. Even though it was more difficult to handle a bank account in seven figures, the fun is gone as I find my Mexican account reduced to something with which I can deal more prosaically. You see, for a few years there, I was a Mexican millionaire, and that's probably the only kind of millionaire I will ever be!

As of this writing, the Mexican government is announcing that new currency is already printed and will be released at the first of 1993. The restaurant menu that now reads 31,000 pesos will read 31.00, and, depending on the exchange rate will transfer into about $10 U.S. And the 4,000,000 pesos in my bank account become a mere 4,000. No fun anymore!

If it is a restaurant check with which you're dealing, remember that the price will be 15% more than quoted on the menu. On all tourist-connected charges there is this value added tax, and it has nothing to do with a tip. It is simply the Mexican government's slice of the dollars that tourists leave in the country. It also applies to such things as fees for homeowners, etc.

Most Gringos do have a local bank account for the sake of convenience. If the unexpected happens and the Gringo runs out of cash, it is not always easy to get a check cashed at your local friendly grocery store. On the contrary, forget it!

Cashing a personal check is not easy in Baja. Banks often charge a minimum of $5 and up to $15 to cash a check on a U.S. bank. Would you believe most merchants would rather have your Visa or Master Card? The only merchants who usually will take checks are the tourist-oriented businesses who also maintain accounts in U.S. banks. They can courier your check across the border and cash it without a penalty.

In fact, even if you have a small account at a Mexican bank, you will usually be charged $5 every time you write a check on your U.S. account to replenish your local account or to get cash; so most Gringos try to provide themselves with cash while in the U.S., even though they have the Mexican account for emergencies.

Either in pesos or dollars, most banks require minimum opening deposit of $1000 U.S. However, with a peso account, one can also have a *cajeta* or card that will work automatic teller machines to get pesos.

Most Gringos I know have small Mexican peso accounts, but some Gringos absolutely refuse! If you want to hear some sad stories sometime, just listen to some of the long time Baja Gringos who had Mexican bank accounts and lost drastically and tragically in past devaluations of the peso.

On the other hand there are those who say that Mexico is the economic miracle of the Third World. Its stock market has shown in the recent past, I'm told, the best performance of any in the entire world. By the time you read this, these statements may not be so; but they may be even more so, and I'm not the one to make predictions. It does seem to me that the old advice about Mexican investments holds good in these times, especially when investing in peso assets. Never invest more than you can afford to walk away from!

Hey, there was also a time when I was receiving more than 40+% interest on those millions of pesos. But that was a time of serious inflation for the Mexican people, and as their economy improves, so does the stability of their money. As it becomes more stable, it is easier to get people to put money into Mexican banks, so they do not have to pay such high interest rates to attract money. Interest as of this writing on my Mexican peso account is 10.7%, and it is about 5% on my dollar account. Those figures may have nothing at all to do with the figures that are current when you read this.

One of the most encouraging signs regarding the Mexican economy is that the Mexicans themselves are investing their own money. Literally hundreds of millions of dollars are going into developments on the Azure Coast of Baja, and the biggest part of it is Mexican investment. In many ways Mexico's economy is getting investors to feel like race horses at the gate, chomping to take off down the economic track. And as in any horse race, there will be winners and losers. A small amount in pesos for the sake of convenience while living in Mexico shouldn't be a much worse bet than $2 on a favorite to show. An even safer bet is a dollar account in one of the local banks, which pays prevailing money market rates.

Business opportunities are apparently opening up to foreigners in Mexico also, but the old "buyer beware" sign is up, I'm sure. There are innumerable unlicensed financial advisors loose in the country these days, and there are also many perfectly ethical stock brokers or attorneys, in Mexico called *licenciados*, who are specialists in the field. But the choice of adviser is not an easy one to make, and the Gringo should probably choose someone recommended by a trusted Mexican friend or stick to the larger, well-established franchise type brokerages.

If the Free Trade Agreement (NAFTA) becomes an accomplished fact, there will be more confidence in the Mexican economy. Most of us Gringos believe the only way things can go is up. But we also recognize that Mexico still has many problems to overcome before the nation can move into economic high gear. As some Mexicans say, "Any decade, now!"

So unless we want the convenience or the "opportunity" of an investment in Mexico, we can get along very well with dollars only. Virtually the only time we cannot deal directly in dollars here in Gringo heaven is when we are paying for something in which the Mexican government is involved. For instance, utilities, which are still for all practical purposes subject to government regulations, put out their bill in pesos and must be paid in same. Therefore it is necessary to go to the bank with dollars and change them into pesos to pay the telephone, electricity or water bills. In addition, sometimes the bill doesn't arrive on time. If it's not paid by due date, there's no excuse. The utility will be discontinued. Recently I heard rumors that the telephone company is changing that policy, but I don't know anyone who has tested it.

These problems explain why so many of us have someone else, usually our insurance agent, whom we pay in dollars, to pay our utility bills for us.

Such things as the resident visa fee, mentioned in a previous chapter, must be paid in pesos, but the drivers of the propane trucks are willing to take dollars. They probably make a few pesos on the side on the exchange.

It is wise, however, to have the correct change for such payments. Few individual Mexicans admit to having change in dollars for small purchases, and change in pesos is something else entirely! Even at the supermarket, you may have to wait while the cashier obtains change for a $20 U.S. bill. Who knows what would happen with a $50 or $100 bill? I try never to have anything larger than a $20, preferably $10, and I always try to keep a good supply of $1 bills on hand.

So you see, we Gringos don't deal in pesos very often, if at all. Two currencies circulate freely in northern Baja, and it is so easy to use the dollars in which we receive our incomes that we seldom bother to change to Mexican money. We're not down here to complicate our lives with unnecessary difficulties; so why make problems when they're not necessary?

15

DO YOU DRINK THE WATER AND EAT THE FOOD DOWN THERE?

Baja too is living in the 20th century, maybe not yet the 21st. Herewith some considerations on hygiene in Baja.

Once upon a time there was a rule that one never ate fresh foods in Mexico unless it was something that could be peeled. And one never, never drank the water or even used it to brush teeth. Well, there may be places in the interior of Mexico where that is still good advice, but in Baja there is little more danger than there is in the U.S.

There are some people who worry about the fact that not all food handlers are licensed and inspected as they are north of the border, and that no one hangs a cleanliness rating sign in a restaurant window in Rosarito, but in most places the rules of hygiene are carefully obeyed. There are laws requiring food handlers to have health cards, and even though Mexican resources do not permit detailed enforcement, most restaurant managers insist on them for their employees, as they do on other rules of hygiene. After all, customers who get sick are hardly a good advertisement for the establishment.

Most of us Baja Gringos go out frequently for dinner or for lunch, and there are no casualties of which we are aware. Granted, we seldom, if ever, patronize the streetside carts, but the established taco stand is certainly on our circuit. We can tell you the ratings on a scale of one to ten of almost every fish taco vendor in our neighborhoods. One of life's goals for some of us is to find the perfect fish taco. In order to be perfect, it must be adorned with fresh cabbage, cilantro, onions, etc., etc., for as much as it will hold! Believe me, if any one of us suffered unpleasantness from such indulgences, the word would soon get around and the vendor would never again have any Gringo business or any other kind in a short time.

As for the good restaurants — and there are many of them — at least those in charge of the kitchen help are now usually trained in hotel schools either in Mexico or in the U.S. Many of the chefs have European training, and few places are in the class of the Mom and Pop establishment anymore. There is a constant upgrading of the kitchen facilities as the businesses grow in Baja, and stainless steel kitchens are becoming standard. The rules of cleanliness are generally carried out as carefully as they are anywhere else. So we all enjoy a crispy salad with our meals. *No problema*!

For those people who worry about the drinking water, there is a great deal of variation in attitudes. There are no water purification facilities in the public supply, but many believe that the water that is delivered through the regular system is probably safe enough. In the northern part of the Azure Coast, it comes from the Colorado River, and new plastic pipes have very recently been installed for the aqueduct. In the lower parts of the area, the water is usually from wells, and since it has been flowing through new pipes also, it too is probably perfectly O.K. to drink. In fact, many Gringos do so. However, water from storage facilities may or may not be drinkable; so the rule of thumb for restaurants is to serve bottled water. Most Gringos also drink the bottled stuff, but most also brush their teeth in tap water. Good bottled water is available in Mexico now, and reverse osmosis water purification systems are being installed in many condo complexes and hotels. Since septic tanks are being abandoned for sewage collection and treatment in new plants, the danger from the drinking water diminishes every day. At any rate, no one seems to have a problem in that regard.

A problem about fresh fruits and vegetables seems much more outdated. Such foods are available in all kinds of stores, from supermarkets to roadside stands, on the Azure Coast. Quality is not always up to the standards that the Gringo is used to and prices are generally the same or a trifle higher than north of the border; so most of us purchase such things in the U.S. For instance, lettuce often is not trimmed, and strawberries are inclined to be smaller and usually riper than we find them in the U.S. However, virtually none of us refuse to purchase in Mexican grocery stores when our supplies run out, and one finds the variety and quality always improving, especially in the larger supermarkets. After all, many of the truck crops that are sold in Southern California supermarkets come from the valleys of Baja, and careful washing is always important in either country.

Good hygiene prevails also in the meat markets and fish stores. Fresh meats and seafoods are available in good variety, and there's many a store where the butcher will cut your meat to order. Your only problem may be buying in kilos instead of pounds. You can end up with more than you want. For instance, don't order half a kilo steak unless you want one that is over a pound all by itself. The kilo is 2.20 pounds, and from experience I know that's a lot of something like *carnitas*! In the supermarkets, meat and chickens are sold packaged, just as in a U.S. market, and none of us hesitate to purchase same when we need meat.

Seafoods are properly iced, and of course they come right out of the sea outside our doors; so they should be fresh. All of us have a favorite place to make such purchases, one that we trust, and of course we always check the appearance and the odor before we walk away with it. When buying cerviche or other raw fish dishes, we make certain we are familiar with the vendor and that there is proper refrigeration available to alleviate our worries.

Frozen foods are beginning to appear in small quantities in the big supermarkets. This seems to say something for the improvements in electrical service as well for hygiene. The first packages looked as if they might not have been kept frozen since packing, but my latest survey found them most attractive, and it seems certain that they will be a regular part of the diet in Baja within a short time.

One worry that we seldom have is insects. So close to the sea there are usually not as many flies as in other places, and the dry countryside seems to discourage most unpleasant insects. It is true that pest control businesses abound as we all have to fight the annual invasion of ants and other such critters that are not discouraged by local conditions. But invasive insects are not as big a problem in regard to the food supply as in other areas.

One problem that can be very unpleasant is public restrooms. Of course, if there is no water, there may be some excuse for unclean facilities. As the water problem alleviates, unclean public restrooms are less and less forgivable, but also less and less common. This writer has a theory. When the restaurant is staffed entirely by men, there is often no one who is willing to do the unpleasant task of cleaning the restrooms, which is often considered only woman's work. And for sure, anyone who doesn't carry a supply of tissues should beware of Mexican restrooms as it is possible there will no paper and towels. At any rate, an unclean restroom always makes me wonder about the kitchen. After all, kitchen cleaning is also considered woman's work.

Is there a problem in swimming in the surf? Well, there are seldom lifeguards on duty, but there are facilities for beach safety as described in the next chapter on medical facilities and emergencies.

The surf is not usually tested along the beaches for health hazards, and the guess of this skeptical Gringa is that it would seldom come up to the standards of U.S. beaches. But many a Gringo surfer has spent much time in the breakers of Baja without any apparent damage to his health, and the beach at Rosarito is crowded on both U.S. and Mexican holidays with no resultant epidemics. "Of course I eat the fish I catch in the surf," a Gringo fisherman told me recently. "Been doing it for fifteen years, and it hasn't hurt me yet!"

In other conditions where hygiene is important, the rules are pretty much the same. There are laws on the books, but they are not always enforced by government. The enforcement depends on the management of the business. For example, my beauty operator, who was trained in the U.S., tells me that such training is not necessary in Baja.

Anybody who wants to can do hair. The shops are supposed to be kept clean under law, but nobody ever comes around to inspect. Therefore it's up to the management to set standards for the skill of the operators and the cleanliness of the premises. For the most part, such facilities adhere to reasonably high standards.

It may be important to mention that the hygiene here described holds true for the developed parts of the cities and in the settled part of the coastline. There are places on hillsides inhabited by virtual squatters where there is no running water, therefore no indoor plumbing, no paved streets, maybe even no electricity, where health conditions are surely more hazardous. And there are many who are concerned about the pollution of hazardous waste, which a poor country like Mexico is unable to afford to control to the extent that the U.S. can. Such problems are not easy for wealthy countries to keep up with. They are much more difficult for Mexico to handle, though extreme efforts are put forth, and progress is being made.

So, for the most part, hygiene is pretty well under control in this little corner of the world. If you're really uncomfortable when you're outside the dubious protection of U.S. sanitary laws, then Mexico is probably not for you. But you probably would never even consider much time in Mexico if you were the kind who couldn't deal with a risk or two here and there! Isn't that so?

16

WHAT HAPPENS IF YOU GET SICK IN BAJA?

In this chapter we will consider some aspects in regard to life and death in Baja. After all, it's not a remote and primitive area, and there are many provisions for good and timely care.

Of course, life is just one thing after another, and for the Baja Gringos, many of whom are at the age where health is becoming less stable and Medicare is the financial lifeline, one of the problems of most concern is medical care. What happens when and if they need emergency medical attention?

First of all, the Gringo can rest assured that Mexican doctors are well trained, intelligent people who are concerned with the patients whom they treat. Many of them, especially the ones who speak English, have had at least some training in the United States. There is absolutely no reason why a Gringo should hesitate to consult a Mexican physician. In fact, he or she is usually more empathetic and frequently more homeopathic in treatment than is the forbidding scientist one usually confronts in the U.S.

As previously mentioned, the same can be said for the Mexican dentist, many of whom are women. Many a U.S. resident comes to Baja for dental care, and most Gringos have their favorite local dentist or *dentista*. For those who require repeated and complicated dental work, the savings can be truly major.

We've already mentioned the drastically lower prices for pharmaceuticals, and there's no question about the fact that unskilled personal care is much more reasonable and dependable than can be found in the U.S.

Nevertheless, there is no comparison to the diagnostic and laboratory facilities that are available to the professionals in the U.S., and hospital and clinic facilities, with some exceptions, are dismal by U.S. standards. There is no sophisticated trauma center available, and few Mexican hospitals offer the decor, let alone the equipment, of U.S. hospitals.

The good news is there is usually minimum equipment to stabilize a traumatically ill patient enough to get him by ambulance across the border. There are a couple of good private hospitals in Tijuana, sometimes working in tandem with San Diego facilities. And there are also a couple of good ones in Rosarito and Ensenada. But they are usually not available to the Gringo in other places on the coast in an emergency. Other hospitals do have emergency facilities, though there is a good deal of variation in such facilities from time to time and place to place.

There is an emergency number like the 911 number north of the border. In Baja it is 134. This will bring a police car, fire engine, or ambulance surprisingly promptly. No *mañana* syndrome at work here. Even if you don't speak Spanish, you may very well find an English speaker on the other end of the telephone. If you are able to ask for an ambulance in Spanish, and the word is very similar (*ambulancia*), you will find yourself in the hands of men (I've never seen a woman in this field) who have had at least some training in caring for emergencies. Many have had extensive training, much of it acquired in U.S. facilities, and some would probably qualify for a paramedic's position north of the border.

The ambulances are clean and just one degree from the latest equipment. Usually they are sold to the Mexican caregivers when a U.S. company up dates its own vehicles, and the Mexican crews take pride in keeping them shiny inside and out.

The Red Cross, the usual emergency facility in Mexico, will probably send the emergency equipment, but private hospitals also have emergency vehicles. Unfortunately, we in Mexico have too often seen these various local private facilities come and go over the years. The Red Cross goes on and on, but it does vary from time to time in regard to what is available to the patients. Finances come from the local population from fees ($4 to see a doctor), social functions, and from local philanthropists, and sometimes the facility simply runs out of funds. Unfortunately there also occasionally has been corruption in the local chapters, and even a little of that evil can cut seriously into the tiny budget upon which they operate. Still, for the most part they are there when needed with adequate facilities.

The ambulance crews are often volunteers, and the policy is that emergency ambulance trips to the border require only a donation of whatever amount is possible. They feel adequately compensated with a donation of $100 or more, depending on distance, time, and the patient's financial capabilities.

There are some horror stories from the past. One concerned a heart patient who was on an ambulance without oxygen. The tank was empty and there was no money to replace it. Another tells of the ambulance stopping somewhere between Rosarito and Tijuana so the crew could visit with some buddies. Sometimes the ambulance drivers have made demands for $100 or more from the patient. In none of these cases was fatality the result, and the repetition of such incidents seems more unlikely all the time as the local Red Cross chapters work so hard to up grade services.

If the ambulance crew is unable to stabilize the

patient, they will take him to a local hospital where surgery and more facilities are available. For most Gringos, stabilization is the key word, with the object being to get the patient as quickly as possible to facilities in the U.S. where Medicare or other health insurance will pay the bills.

Medicare will pay only for emergency care in an accident when the patient is traveling in Mexico. Therefore the major concern of the Gringo is emergency care and transportation. Many HMOs or supplemental insurance plans will cover Mexican care to some extent. I know Gringos in Ensenada who have had even elective surgery there which was paid for entirely by insurance supplemental to Medicare. But it is up to the Gringo to find out the rules of his particular carrier. Incidentally, if the patient depends on Medicaid or state financed care, it will be denied to a full-time resident of Baja.

There are a few Gringos who are not old enough to be covered by Medicare or affluent enough to have good U.S. health insurance. Some of them will swear by the medical treatment they received under local doctors and in hospitals, and the cost for such is probably one-quarter or less of what they would have paid in the U.S. One reason may be that in many local hospitals it is necessary to have family to bring meals and to provide personal care such as baths. The bigger, Gringo-oriented hospitals in Tijuana and Ensenada provide such services to patients.

Many an ill Gringo is transported to the border by his own family, and it is usually not necessary to drag through the border lines. If the driver will pull up to any empty gate and flash his lights, someone will come within a very short time to take care of the problem. At very busy times, the far right gate is reserved for emergencies and buses.

On the other hand, there are stories of marvelous international cooperation, where a U.S. ambulance was allowed into Mexico to pick up a Gringo or where the Mexican ambulance was allowed to transport the patient all the way to a U.S. hospital without waiting at the border for a change of transport. Such events are probably illegal, but they come about as the two nations' caregivers and authorities look the other way when a life is at stake.

There is an active international network of emergency and rescue services. Law enforcement officers of both nations meet frequently as do such groups as pilots, coast guard, etc. There are times when a U.S. Coast Guard helicopter, for instance, can get permission to fly in Mexican territory to pick up an injured seaman. Private pilots as well as private air evacuation services have little problem in arranging mercy flights for injured or seriously ill Gringos, even into the interior of the peninsula. Search and rescue teams are usually made up of men and facilities from both sides of the border, and there is the Binational Emergency Medical Care Committee in Chula Vista to coordinate the efforts for Gringo evacuation and care in emergencies.

At some beaches, at some times, there are life guards available. Their service depends on the financial capabilities of the municipality that is supposed to provide them. There are rescue units of various kinds available in the peninsula. Most of these are volunteers, but they are devoted and usually capable. One such outfit is the *Rescate Halcones* or Rescue Hawks who fly ultra-light planes over the various beaches.

Obviously, things are not too bad for you if you are injured or become ill in Baja, but life can be pretty difficult for your survivors if you die there! You'll cause a slew of problems for your family! Dead bodies require lots of papers that must be rubber stamped by various officials, and no Gringo survivor should attempt the procedure without a Spanish-speaking friend. Some widows have used their insurance agents, but the U.S. Consulate is available to help at such a time. One thing that will make such an untoward event somewhat easier is the deceased's prior registration with the U.S. Consulate. In any case, the Consulate must be contacted to provide the equivalent of a U.S. death certificate to use for legalities there.

There was a time when cremation was almost impossible to obtain in Mexico, but it is now available in several places on the Azure Coast and at a price less than it would be across the border. If, however, the body is to be transported across the border, expense and red tape add to the problems of the family, and once again the U.S. Consulate is the best expediter.

In fact, there are several numbers that the Gringo should have with him at all times in case of accident or illness. One is that of the U.S. Consulate, which has phones in Tijuana and a 24-hour number in the U.S. (81-7400 in Tijuana; 619-585-2000 in San Diego). Another number the Gringo should carry is that of his insurance agent. Sometimes such a person is able to vouch for the insurance or the integrity of an incarcerated Gringo.

The third essential number is that of the Binational Emergency Medical Care Committee in Chula Vista, a nongovernment, nonprofit agency, to expedite transportation in case of illness. Call (619) 425-5080.

Actually, from the standpoint of emergency health care, the Gringo is probably as well off as he would be in most places in the U.S. It isn't like living next door to a hospital or fire station, but the chances of survival and recovery are probably almost as good as they would be in any such situation in the U.S. And you can be sure it won't cost as much!

CAN GRINGOS OWN PROPERTY IN BAJA?

The answer is "No," but really it's "Yes." Herewith we consider the Mexican property laws as they apply on the Azure Coast.

There's no question that the Mexican government is becoming more tolerant, yes, even eager, to encourage foreign investment in the country. Yet there are many potential investors among whom the feelings of distrust die hard. After all, Mexico has a long history of corrupt bureaucracy and anti-American prejudices. Even in the 19th century, Mexicans themselves who had land grants from the government more than once found themselves in Mexico City trying to bribe the bureaucrats into allowing them to maintain their properties. In the early part of this century there was such a backlash against "Yankee Imperialists" that American property was confiscated in the 1930s, and laws were passed forbidding foreigners to own land within 100 kilometers of the border and within 50 kilometers of the coast, which affected virtually all of Baja.

As the world enters the 21st century, it is obvious that attitudes are changing throughout the world, and that includes Mexico. The government has been stable since 1910, and though there are many changes taking place in the nation, revolution does not seem imminent. The free market is being encouraged, and many former government operations are being sold to private enterprises. A proposed free trade zone, including Canada and the U.S., seems imminent at this writing, and, if consummated, will surely be an enormous stimulus to the economy of the country. *Mordida*, or in English bribery, if not yet eliminated, seems to be becoming less flagrant. Such trends are making the acquisition of property, even in the coastal and border zones, more attractive for those who would settle in the area.

Before we proceed with this discussion, please understand that I am not a lawyer in either country. This chapter is based on careful research, but it is not intended as a substitute for your own lawyer. In spite of whatever feelings we may have personally about that profession, lawyers are often a necessity to guide us through the maze of U.S. laws, and they are probably even more essential in a foreign country where the laws are written in a language that most of us cannot even read. The wise Gringo feels a need for a lawyer, and some hire such counsel in Mexico. Others will tell you that it is better to deal with a U.S. lawyer who knows both countries' laws to make certain that your assets are protected in both countries. In any case, this chapter is intended as only a superficial overview of what the potential Gringo investor can expect.

In spite of the prohibition against direct foreign ownership of property virtually anywhere in Baja California, there is a provision that makes it possible for the Gringo to have most rights of ownership. Long term trusts, called *fideicomisos*, under the trusteeship of banks, are available and in most ways are a perfectly acceptable alternative to outright ownership.

The *fideicomisos* came about as the result of serious horror stories of U.S. citizens who had been taken by unscrupulous souls who promised them 99-year leases and other privileges not available under Mexican law, and then absconded with the money and left the Gringos in total disaster. Such con men also sold the Gringos land on the beaches, which are owned exclusively by the federal government. Nobody, but *NOBODY* can own land within 20 meters (about 65 feet) of the mean high tide line, or in some places, the top of the cliffs above that line. So some Gringos found themselves thinking they owned property where only the feds could have title.

In view of these various scams, the Mexican government in 1973 passed a law setting up the *fideicomiso* or bank trust to eliminate such shenanigans on the part of dishonest real estate operators.

Since the legal title of the property cannot be in the name of a foreigner, it resides in the name of the bank who holds it in trust for the named "beneficiary," or the person who owns the equity. Such trusts are written for a maximum of 30 years, and they are administered by the bank. When this approach is used, it virtually eliminates the dishonest operator as the title must be clear, and the trust must be in accordance with Mexican law.

As the law was originally written, it required that the *fideicomiso* be sold at the end of its term to a Mexican national, and when the original trusts began to reach mid-point, there developed much speculation on the bad scenarios that could come about when the 30 years were up. Just imagine the unscrupulous Mexicans running about buying up property for a song that could no longer be sold to other Gringos and could not be kept by the original purchaser.

But the bad scenario has been virtually eliminated since the law has been changed to allow such trusts to be renewed for an additional 30 years. A lot of people feel that when that second 30 years gets close to expiration beginning in 2033, there will be more expansion of the law to provide more advantages of the free market. And for those who are making such bank trusts in the 1990s, expiration will not come about before the 2050s. Who knows what economical and social changes will have taken place by then?

After the original purchase, the beneficial owner pays a service charge, varying from one-quarter of 1% to 2% of the purchase price for the property, every year for the administration of the trust by the bank. However, please remember that as the value of the property increases, reassessments can take place, and the annual fee can increase. In some cases recently, the *fideicomiso* fees took drastic jumps, and homeowners have had to go to the trouble of reinstituting the trust in a competing bank which offered lower fees.

There is no security of title to compare with what you expect in the United States. Theoretically, the *fideicomiso* is supposed to take care of that, providing a Certificate of Freedom from Liens, but if something is missed in the process, there's no one to take care of it except the owner. Here's where a good lawyer can again be of help. It is possible to buy U.S. title insurance on Mexican property, but it's very expensive.

The beneficial owner has all rights of succession or sales and all others that go with ownership for the duration of the trust. It is even possible to include the names of heirs at the time the trust is taken out, which will avoid probate upon the death of the original beneficiary. Watch out for unexpected restrictions as to what can be built or installed. Be aware of such before you make the deal.

There is another caveat in regard to the *fideicomisos*. The one renewable for the additional 30 years is one that is irrevocable. There is another kind which cannot be renewed unless the seller wishes to renew it. It is called a revocable trust and usually applies to such properties as time shares or mobile home parks. Make certain you are aware of which kind you are obtaining!

Of course, there are costs for setting up such a trust, at this writing from about $1000 up, depending on the value of the property and including the first year's administration fees. The Gringo can work directly with the bank or, with a clear understanding ahead of time on the additional costs involved, through a lawyer or a reliable real estate agent. Since all paperwork must be in Spanish, the average Gringo will have to have some Mexican contact to deal with that problem at least.

Notice the stress on the word *reliable* in connection with real estate agents. There is no provision for licensing such dealers in Mexico, but there are several ways for the Gringo to be relatively sure of the integrity of the agent with whom he is dealing. One way is to find one who is a member of A.M.P.I. (Mexican Nationwide Association of Realtors), an organization that holds its members to high standards of knowledge and ethics. Another alternative is to deal with firms franchised by U.S. companies, such as Century 21 and others.

Additional expenses during the cost of the lease of course include real estate taxes, about 1½% of the purchase price, and in most developments, homeowner's fees. Brace yourself also for the 15% IVA or value added tax tacked onto almost all such bills.

There are those who believe the consumer is inadequately protected in Mexico, and surely there are fewer safeguards than in a country like the U.S. Reliable Mexican professionals provide some protection for the consumer, but there are government agencies that are on hand to help the consumer avoid trouble with a realtor, contractor or seller. There are two agencies, the State Attorney General for the Protection of Tourism and the Federal District Attorney's Office for the Protection of the Consumer available at no charge. Both provide such services as checking of contracts by bilingual attorneys and some efforts at redress of grievances.

It is wise to take the precaution of never paying in full for any transaction until you are satisfied that everything is in order. This is where a good lawyer or reliable real estate agent is so important. You will probably also want a good English translation of any sales documents. Make sure all taxes have been paid to the date of transfer of property, including the seller's taxes. Yes, the seller's taxes. Collection is made from any source available in Mexico. Here is where that Certificate of Freedom from Liens is so important!

There are real cynics who insist that in Mexico one should never invest more than he can afford to walk away from, and there are others who believe that the real estate boom is just getting under way, and that appreciation will be a major factor in the future. This writer advises that of course, the buyer should beware and be very careful and get good advice, but that *investment* is not the key word for property in Mexico. *Enjoyment* is what the Gringo is seeking in Mexican property.

Find a place you can be comfortable with physically and financially and use good judgement and good advice in the arrangements. Then relax and enjoy it! The purpose of purchasing property in Mexico is for the enjoyment of visiting or living there, and none of us can tell what the future will bring even in the U.S. If the future is somewhat more uncertain in Mexico, so be it! It's no longer really dangerous or hopeless, and it might even be great!

18

DOES ANYBODY IN HIS RIGHT MIND EVER TRY TO BUILD A HOUSE IN MEXICO?

It is possible to build your dream home on the Azure Coast, but there are some caveats that must be kept in mind.

There are lots of happy homeowners who had their places built in Mexico, and they almost all say that there is good news and the possibility of bad news for anyone who wants to undertake such a project. Mr. and Mrs. Gringo can build their dream home in northern Baja California, but it requires some care and attention.

The happy homeowners are, first, the ones who are under the protection of a *fideicomiso*. Agreement is almost unanimous that no major expense should be undertaken without the *fideicomiso*. Virtually any other arrangement is subject to too many hazards to justify spending the cost of the home. Also no part of your house should sit on federal lands. You will have to pay rent every year to the federal government, and the law is hazy about who owns the entire house if any part of it encroaches on federal beaches.

Secondly, look for a high quality contractor. Even in the U.S. this is often a complicated problem. In Mexico the complication is even greater because there is no licensing of contractors and because prices vary so much from one to another. There are some brave Gringo souls who build without a contractor, but they may find themselves with some indefinable problems from time to time.

People with clipboards appear requiring expensive changes that can be avoided with the payment of money. Special permits may be required which have expense attached to them. A Mexican contractor knows the real expenses entailed and figures such expenses into his price. Often, though not always, the more expensive one will provide more services, such as architectural drawings, etc.

Almost all authorities agree that nothing should be started precipitously. If the potential builder is not already a resident of the area, a visit of several months in the area is advised. Talk to lots of people. Probably one of the best ideas is to join one of the local societies such as the United Society of Baja California and seek out those who have already gone through the process of building. Ask about their contractors and why each was chosen. Look at the results. This may be the most important decision you will make in regard to your home, so take time to choose carefully.

When you are familiar with some interesting prospects as contractors, talk to them in detail. Ask to see other things he has built and to talk to the owners. Go to the contractor's home to see what he has done for himself. Does he specialize in *negro* contracting (basic construction) or *blanco* contracting (finish construction)? Talk about price per square foot and total costs.

There are all kinds of arrangements that can be made. You might want to have the *negro* construction done, and finish the details yourself or with the help of available unskilled labor. You might want to work from virtually any kind of pre-prepared plans to get the necessary permits and then add on as you go along. You can hire a Mexican architect to prepare your plans, or you might want to deal with one of the more expensive contractors who will draw plans to your specifications before you make the contract for construction. Whatever arrangements you make will depend on your own skills and capabilities.

Be sure to think of everything you want. Extra wiring including 220? Central heat? Size of rooms? And keep in mind that the word "standard" in Mexico represents entirely different criteria than in the United States. A standard bedroom in Mexico is probably about ten feet by ten feet. To a Mexican contractor a standard light fixture may well be a ceramic fixture into which a bulb can be screwed. In many cases, the home builder insists on buying his own fixtures in the United States and bringing them south. It is surely possible to purchase them in Mexico, often for a somewhat lower price, but it is probably easier to find them in the U.S. Most Gringos agree that many aspects of the home will have to be upgraded from Mexican standards. Of course, that will add to the price, but usually such changes are not expensive.

Don't do business on a handshake in Mexico any more than you would in the United States. A contract is an absolute necessity, written in both Spanish and English, and preferably signed by a notary, that all-important official in Mexico. Then you may use the Mexican courts to enforce the contract. However, believe me, the Mexican courts are truly a last resort.

The contract should spell out what will be accomplished for each payment made, and payment should be doled out in rather small increments, say $5000 at a time, because sadly, even well-known contractors have been known to abandon a job and disappear. They are not bonded in Mexico. Make the contract as explicit as possible, but remember that, even more than in other places in the world, its success will depend considerably on the rapport between the parties involved.

It is almost unanimously agreed that the homeowner should not be an absentee builder. Almost daily visits are advised to inspect and inquire about what is going on. For instance one day you arrive at the construction scene to find men starting to dig a new hole. You'd better ask, "What is that hole the men have begun to dig next to the septic tank? It's the what? The *pila*, the cistern for water storage? No, no! That must be put as far away as possible! Dig it at the other end of the house!" Get the picture? In Mexico there are no building inspectors to enforce certain quality as the building is being done. The owner must be his own inspector and enforce the standards that he wants in the building. Within reason, he can even insist on the order in which the work is done.

If the owner is not knowledgeable enough to supervise carefully, then he simply must have a contractor with whom he has a good understanding or hire someone he trusts to supervise for him. A good understanding is often complicated by a language barrier unless one or both parties are very fluent in and can conduct their business in one language or another. Otherwise, sometimes they may think they understand each other but have really misunderstood. Another reason for a careful watch over what is happening.

Mexican workers are becoming more skilled all the time, and their tools are constantly being upgraded. On larger projects at least, pre-mixed concrete trucks are replacing the wheelbarrows and shovels that too often resulted in by-guess-and-by-gosh concrete. One sometimes hears power saws now, though so far I've never heard an electric hammer. The pay for workers who have some degree of skill is also improving, although it remains cheaper to hire unskilled labor from among the immigrants from the interior of the country; so a job like the breaking of concrete is usually still done by chisel and sledge hammer, and most digging is done with shovels.

When it comes to home building south of the border, many a Baja lover has been influenced by Jack Smith's famous book on building a home in Baja, *God and Mr. Gomez*. We Baja Gringos have always loved the book because he captured so beautifully the Mexican spirit of caring, in their own inimitable ways, for the welfare of the Gringos with whom they have developed a rapport. It is not applicable now to the part of the peninsula called the Azure Coast, though any prospective Baja Gringo should read it. It was written some years ago and dealt with an area where things remain more difficult, farther south than the Azure Coast. For anyone but the most naive builder, conditions are much different today in northern Baja *frontera*. Mr. and Mrs. Gringo can build their dream home now for less than one-half the price it would cost in the U.S. and feel happy and comfortable in it. But careful vigilance is part of the price that must be paid.

19

WHAT IS THERE TO DO WITH YOUR TIME IN BAJA?

People who have spent their entire lives in crowded cities often wonder what we semi-expatriates do with ourselves in Baja. Turns out that's no problem for us.

Some of my friends have a hard time understanding my life in Baja. "But when you're not writing," say my incredulous Stateside friends, "what do you do down there?" Since they know I'm not the strenuous outdoor type, they think there's nothing for me to do but to sit and watch the waves roll in, which really isn't all that bad a way to spend some time. But the fact is that anybody who wants to spend time that way will have to arrange to take the time from other goings-on in the area.

"Do!" I exclaim to those who question me on that problem. "Why, there's more to do and more sharing of good friendships than you will ever find in most metropolitan areas."

Most people think of Baja for its fishing, off-road events, surfing, horseback riding, and all those other great outdoor activities that have made it such a popular tourist spot for so many years. But many of those of us who are regular residents have passed the strenuous part of our lives. A brisk walk along the beach or a hot game of golf is about as strenuous as most of us get. Oh, there are those who play tennis frequently, and some of us live in or belong to facilities where a swimming pool or gym is available, but for the most part, most of us prefer less physical activities and more comfortable recreation. Frankly, I have never seen one of my fellow residents carrying a surfboard. So what do we do?

Well, it all depends on how much activity we want. Those who like an active social life can literally spend every single day of the week enjoying the companionship of other Gringos in various activities. Many of such doings are part of the various philanthropic or social organizations in which the full or part time residents are involved. Some are the proceedings of the various condo complexes, and some are just the informal arrangements between friends with similar interests who share with each other in their homes or at the popular bistros. The only limit on the social lives of the residents is the one they impose upon themselves!

The largest organized activities take place in the organizations that U.S. citizens have set up in the area. There's a large organization called the United

Society of Baja California in Rosarito Beach which has over 300 members, and there are two such organizations in Ensenada, the *Vecinos de Punta Banda* and the *Amigos de Ensenada*.

There are equally active groups of women who form an important part of fund raising for Mexican charities of various kinds. Perhaps the most active is the auxiliary to the local Red Cross, which in Mexico is one of the primary health care providers for the local citizenry. The local female Gringas provide an important part of that organization's fund-raising program in coordination with the Mexican women. Fashion shows, balls, days at the races, and the operation of a thrift shop are all part of their activities. Other groups of women work to raise funds for other worthy causes. Just how much charity work does a gal want to do?

The United Society in Rosarito and the Ensenada groups also provide an active social life, with weekly sessions of all kinds of card and board games and with bridge lessons along with party bridge and duplicate. The organizations have general meetings usually once a month in which speakers are invited to talk about everything from what's going on in the communities to the art scene in the area. Laws, health care, new services in almost any field, charity workers, as well as any other aspect of life that affects the Mexican community and the Gringos in it are part of the monthly programs. They also provide some funding for local charity organizations and take part in civic affairs as much as possible.

The boards of directors are busy groups, but even the ordinary members find that decisions must be made as to which activities should be indulged in.

Monthly pot lucks invite participation, along with special events for holidays like Mother's Day or Fourth of July. There are weekly breakfasts, monthly or weekly dine-outs and luncheons. You like deep sea fishing, literary discussions, golf? All are planned for your enjoyment. Want to take Spanish lessons or art lessons? They too are arranged for members. If you're a traveler, there are group tours for various places from Las Vegas to the Caribbean, and, if there's some ham in you, you can get involved as an actor or a member of the stage crew in little theatre. Just how much fun do you want to have?

Mexican businesses and government agencies seem always anxious to cooperate with the Gringo organizations, providing facilities for meetings and other functions and English language speakers for meetings. There is much cooperation between the Mexican and American communities, and people of both nations meet for mutual problem solving.

And then there are all the things going on that are not related to any particular social organizations. Health and recreation centers are beginning to appear providing such activities as aerobics, dance lessons, Spanish and English lessons, swimming pools, racquetball and other kinds of activities for families or individuals, both Gringo and Mexican. Some such facilities are also offered in the various condo complexes; so there's no excuse for any of us to be out of condition, even if we aren't the outdoors type.

And then there are the walks, so much a part of living in Baja. With such an equable climate, it is seldom too hot or too chilly to enjoy a walk on the beach or to almost any other place one has to go. Even women alone do not hesitate to walk wherever they please, even after dark.

If the scheduled attractions are not enough there are always individuals who open their homes, who invite their friends for parties, games and other activities. There are also the informal social engagements, partaking of the marvelous restaurants in the area or enjoying the piano bars or dining and dancing opportunities.

And always the public events such as seafood festivals, Mexican holiday celebrations, bicycle rides, contests on the beach and other goings on are available to enjoy either by taking part in the fun or by watching when the spirit moves you.

In addition, we almost all allow some time to return to the States to do some shopping or visit doctors or family, whatever is part of our lives up there. It's not far to go for a special celebration or for a special event such as opera or a baseball game. Anything that is important to us farther north does not need to be neglected, and most of us have to find time for such trips, though we often find them a nuisance. Often we hate to give up what we have going in Baja.

So when my friends ask, "What do you do?" — the answer is we do everything, or, if we prefer, we do nothing but watch the waves roll in. Baja is a place where everyone does his or her own thing. You will be welcomed when you partake of community activities, or accepted if you prefer privacy from time to time. Whatever you do with your time in Baja is strictly up to you — busy or idle — athlete or couch potato — philanthropist or iconoclast — social butterfly or loner. Find your niche and slide into it. There's plenty — or nothing — for all to do!

20

WHAT KIND OF CULTURAL OR ARTISTIC LIFE DOES BAJA OFFER?

A cultural wasteland, Baja is not! In which we take a quick look at the possibilities for the Gringo to enjoy the more esoteric pastimes available in big U.S. cities.

One of the pleasures of living on the Azure Coast is that the Gringo is not isolated from activities that he is used to. A trip into San Diego, one of the seven largest cities in the U.S., is less than an hour away except for the border crossing. So everything the person is used to doing can still be accomplished without too much difficulty.

In fact, there are several suburbs of San Diego that are less than ten minutes from the border crossing: San Ysidro, Chula Vista, Imperial Beach, and National City. Many a Gringo has a post office box in one of those cities, and when crossing the border to pick up mail, also goes to the library or to one of the big shopping malls. Some belong to senior centers in one of those cities and go there to do things that they enjoy when such activities are not going on in Baja.

Busloads of Baja Gringos often take off to see the Padres or the Chargers play in San Diego, and when such events as America's Cup races, Superbowls, or All-Star games take place in San Diego, you can be sure those Gringos who are interested get there without too much effort. Sometimes busloads are organized for such events in more distant cities, and the border crossing becomes unimportant when the bus driver is the one handling the border lines.

With the new diamond lanes at the border, it is not uncommon for four Gringos to carpool and cross the border relatively easily for such functions as golf games on San Diego courses or for cultural events like operas or symphonies, or the theater. Seldom does one get a busload for the more esoteric affairs, but it is not a difficult drive home after an evening performance in San Diego. Busloads are frequently organized for functions farther afield such as Broadway musicals in Los Angeles or something like the Pageant of the Masters at Laguna Beach. Whatever the Gringo misses from his life in a U.S. city is available easily from his home on the Azure Coast.

Yet anyone who thinks that it is necessary to head across the border to enjoy some of the culture of life just simply doesn't realize what a Mexican city like Tijuana has to offer. This place is anything but a cultural wasteland! On the contrary, it's full of interesting things to see and do even for those who cannot understand the Spanish language.

The best known place to keep up with the cultural scene in Tijuana is the famous Centro de Cultura on the Paseo de los Heroes in Tijuana. Here is a fine auditorium as well as a dome projection theater, a fine museum, and rotating art exhibits. A variety of performers from rock bands to the Mexican National Symphony appear in the auditorium, and many of them are enjoyable in whatever language.

There is, however, one major problem involved, especially for us Gringos. It seems bookings are made not far in advance at such places in Mexico, and the only notice we get of coming events is when we drive past the marquee in the traffic circle outside the Cultural Center. Of course we're handling the traffic, trying to read dates and times in Spanish, and, since the current function is what is announced, we are usually disappointed to find it is closing before we can get there. Even the Mexican newspapers don't seem to usually know in advance. There is one newspaper in Tijuana, *Zeta*, that sometimes has the word a week ahead on what's going on, but that newspaper is in Spanish; so few of us buy it regularly. Actually a week's notice seems to be about the best we can expect in either language.

Monthly stops by the Center are well worth it to see the interesting visual arts shows they mount there. Artists from all over Mexico are attracted to this corner of the country for the market afforded by the proximity to the U.S. and by the large number of Mexicans who can not only afford a house and furniture, but can also begin to decorate it as well. Mexico, which has a proud artistic tradition from the time of the Aztecs and Mayans, is producing some really fine painters and sculptors, many of whom are settling in north-western Baja. Rosarito Beach particularly is seen as the future heart of a dynamic artistic development! These artists are frequently shown at the Cultural Center as well as in private galleries in Tijuana, Rosarito, and in Ensenada. Some of the most exciting art in the world is being created on the Azure Coast.

Many Mexican artists in all fields are coming out of the Casa de Cultura in Tijuana as well as from the state university campuses in Baja Norte. Training is offered at the pre-university level at the Casa de Cultura for artists, dancers, musicians, and other practitioners of the performing arts. The results include very well trained dancers in all forms from Mexican *folklorico*, whose dancers obviously have had ballet training, to modern revues. There is even a ballet troupe in Mexicali that has performed in San Diego with good reviews. The future of dance promises to be exciting in Baja.

This writer is not prepared to comment on Mexican theater because it is beyond the ken of a non-Spanish speaker, but among those who can enjoy it, the local productions are reported as excellent. And there is a struggling Baja California Symphony, made up of émigres from the former Soviet Union, small but first rate. We are all ardently hoping that it will not flounder financially.

In addition to the Mexican cultural scene, there are many Gringos who add to the artistic scene in the border community. Retired artists from all over the country find inspiration in the landscapes and way of life in Baja. And dozens of people do free lance writing more or less seriously. Serious readers also are abundant, and they love to get together to talk about what they've read.

Other aspects of cultural life are not ignored on the Azure coast. Religion is an important part of the life of many Gringos. Catholics usually attend the local churches, and many offer at least one mass on Sundays in English. Protestant churches are usually interdenominational, and there are many of them throughout the area. This writer does not know of any Eastern religious congregations, which is not to say there are none. Surely the foreign managers of the *maquiladoras* have places of worship, but if not, they probably go to San Diego where virtually all religions are represented.

In other words, a cultural wasteland Baja Norte is not! If what is going on locally is not exciting enough for you, it's easy to wheel off to San Diego or points north for anything that's important for you to see!

21

WHAT KIND OF PEOPLE ARE THE BAJA GRINGOS?

All kinds, just like anywhere else, is the first thought. But are they perhaps different in some ways? Let's examine who is there and why.

"We found our home in Southern California had appreciated beyond our wildest dreams, and we found the neighborhood had changed. Friends and neighbors had left, and crime was increasing. We had been coming to Ensenada on vacations since our children were small; so we sold our home, invested the bulk of the money, and built our dream home on the hills overlooking Ensenada. Now we have enough money from our investments to care for ourselves in comfort for the rest of our lives." Such is a typical scenario of many of the Gringos.

Or, "I work for a company in the U.S. as a salesman in Tijuana and Tecate. Rather than commute every day, I prefer to live down here," says a young neighbor, "and many managers of the *maquiladoras* that I contact also live in this area."

"I came down here because I could see my retirement would not permit me to live as I would like to in the U.S.," says a widow in Rosarito. "As prices go up here in Baja, it's not as good as it used to be, but it's still better than I could do further north."

Another Gringo told me, "I have a terrible dread of going to a nursing home. Down here it is still possible to get affordable personal care in my own home. As long as possible I intend to remain on my own."

"I came to be far enough away from my children and grandchildren so they couldn't call on me for something every day, but not so far that it would be really difficult to get together with them."

"I have always loved Baja and Mexico. Now I can live wherever I please. I choose to live here."

"I came down here looking for a wealthy Mexican cowboy."

Those are just some of the scenarios of the Gringos who are here, though I don't think it would be true to say the last one is very typical. There are probably dozens of others, because people live in Baja for all kinds of reasons.

First of all, a large percentage of them are retired. Few people in their working years can obtain employment in Mexico, and for others the border commute is forbidding. That *doesn't* mean that only senior citizens make up the Gringo population. Neighbors within the writer's *campo* include at least half a dozen working people, either in Mexico or as employees of a U.S. company who work in Mexico or commute. And there are those of us who write or paint or do other free lance work either before or after retirement age.

It's safe to say that most Gringos, though not by any means all, do not speak Spanish, and the resulting lack of communication can lead to some social problems. It is difficult to take part in, let's say, the local historical society, when most members are dealing with the subject in a language that is incomprehensible to even the most interested participant. The subtleties and innuendos, for sure, as well as many of the actual happenings in the political structure, are beyond the Gringo's comprehension unless he or she is very fluent indeed in Spanish.

Some Mexicans resent the fact that the Gringos do not learn the language of their adopted country, and even those who feel no animosity are inclined to avoid the problems caused by translation, explanation, etc., for the non-Spanish speaker. After all, they have other things to do than explain the complications of the proceedings to someone with virtually no understanding of what is going on!

Yet this unilingualism is an uniting factor for the Gringo community. In some ways they are isolated from the activities of the city around them; so they have more time to put into the activities of the Gringo community. If a Gringo becomes part of the general social scene in Baja by joining one of the Gringo organizations or one of the binational organizations like the *Cruz Roja* (Red Cross), that Gringo soon becomes familiar to everyone else in the English speaking community, and, in some ways, he or she becomes a valued member of a small town. Everybody knows everybody else and knows all their secrets. So the community is like a small town with all the care for each other, with the well known leaders, with the comfortable social functions, with a common knowledge about others' lives.

But there is where the resemblance to small town U.S. seems to come to an end. Everyone may know, but no one criticizes. So Suzie may be an alcoholic. When the liver gives out, there is someone there to take her to the U.S. to the hospital. So Joe and Josie are living together without benefit of marriage. Who cares? On the other hand, so-and-so may be as nutty as the proverbial fruit cake, and though people may try to avoid him, they certainly would never interfere with his activities unless he was interfering with theirs.

"People here are much more tolerant," one of my Gringa friends told me when I said that we were just like people everywhere, and she pointed out to me that only those who have some sense of adventure would ever consider living here in the first place. It may well be true that there has to be an element of nonconformism in those who are willing to become semi-expatriates. She insists that those with different interests are accepted, neither ridiculed nor held in awe. In fact, the only Gringos who have a hard time fitting into the local society are those who arrive with preconceived ideas of right and wrong and who try to impose such ideas on those around them.

Of course, they all come from somewhere else. They are all immigrants. Many of them come from the southwestern part of the United States, though there are many who come from the East Coast or from Canada. There are the full-timers and the part-timers and the weekenders.

The weekenders appear for some special function such as a bicycle race or an off-road activity and have little contact with the actual community. Some have been arriving frequently for a number of years, have regular friends in the area, and are almost like part-timers or full-timers.

Then there are the part-timers, those who come from places like Denver or the Dakotas for the winter. Or there's another half of them who come from the California desert areas, Arizona, or the eastern and central parts of California for the summer. Some come in the winter to avoid extreme cold; some come in the summer to avoid extreme summer temperatures. What does that tell you about the climate of the area? The part-timers often own condos in the area, and are welcomed back to their usual activities with warmth and affection by those whom they have not seen for the past season.

But of course it is the full-timers who really maintain the on-going community functions year after year. It is they who form the core of the community for better or for worse, becoming regular members of boards of directors in Gringo organizations and creating new activities and interests.

Financial situations vary considerably. There are some very wealthy, but we may not know who they are. Clothes and local activities are pretty much the same for all, and what is done outside of the area is seldom discussed in detail. Most are probably living with some degree of comfort with decent retirement incomes on which they do better in Baja than in communities farther to the north. There are some on really seriously short incomes, but even they can usually manage to keep up with the usual social activities of the community.

The better off give dinner parties for each other; those with moderate incomes go to Gringo social functions and sometimes take part in travels or group activities north of the border. The financially strapped maintain a social life with pot luck dinners, bridge or other social games, church activities, and other inexpensive past times. Few of us mark the differences.

We have our share of the formerly famous, a retired OSS man, a retired TV star, artists, writers, etc. There are a surprising number who possess advanced college degrees, and some whose education may be less than they would prefer. Again, no one makes very much of all of this. There is a compatibility made up of similar interests and of similar isolation in a foreign community that makes camaraderie more important than background.

There are a few who still seem to believe that they are doing the Mexicans a favor by investing and living in the country. Though at some time in the past that may have been true, it certainly is not any longer. The Mexican middle class is growing fast, and the Gringos are becoming less important every day in the economy of the area. Yet there are those who insist as prices rise that the Mexicans are trying to exploit the Gringos. There still seem to be some antediluvians who have no respect for Mexicans and seem to believe that they are all either corrupt or stupid. Some have never had a Mexican as a guest in their homes nor ever visited in a Mexican home.

This parochialism can sometimes result in unpleasantness between the two communities. For example, the Gringo community may donate money for a specific need and some among the donors will try to dictate to the Mexicans in detail how they must spend the money. Usually those who engage in such actions do so because they really believe the Mexicans are incapable of making reasonable decisions for themselves. Such attitudes can be most insulting to the local authorities.

Yet most Gringos are aware of the desperate needs caused by the poverty of those who immigrate to the area from the interior of Mexico, and there are many Gringos who are very active in charity affairs. Many give freely in small amounts and some in larger amounts to try to ameliorate some of the conditions that they see around them. Gringas work long, hard hours in the Red Cross thrift shop as well as contributing to fund raisers of all kinds. Barbecues and hot dog sales are a part of the Gringo participation in various charity affairs. The little theater group donates profits to various needy organizations throughout the community, and individuals work through their church groups or otherwise to help where they can, usually without trying to tell the Mexicans how to run their affairs.

Many Gringos truly admire and respect the Mexican culture and try to learn all they can about it and adhere to its traditions when dealing with its people. Surely they are the Gringos who are welcome in the community.

One of the best things about the community is that the resident is really free to take part as much or as little as he or she likes. One can become part of the little core group; or one can ignore them and make friends in his own complex or even go across the border for social life. The Gringo has true social freedom in Baja and as much or as little participation as he wishes, with a large variety of people and functions from which to choose.

Yes, there are all kinds of people among the Gringo community is Baja, but it does seem accurate to say that the person who is rigid in attitudes about what other people should do or who is timid about facing different approaches to living probably does not belong in Mexican Baja. Therefore, we find comparatively few of them in the Gringo *campos* of the Azure Coast.

22

WHICH OF ALL THOSE BEAUTIFUL SPOTS SHOULD I CHOOSE?

You've decided you want to join us, but you don't know where to start looking. Herewith a few thoughts about the good and the problems with the various campos or complexes.

So now you've decided you'd like to be a Baja Gringo, and you begin to look for the ideal spot for your future home. Beautiful seaside or hillside lots are all around you at various prices. Which should you choose?

As previously indicated, your interests in life will have much influence on your decision. Again let's take the trip from north to south down the coast, considering some of the pitfalls and pleasures in the various locations.

Tijuana itself is not very often chosen as a homesite for the usual Baja Gringo, but parts of it might be very satisfactory for an executive of a twin plant. There are some lovely homes in that city with spectacular views, and other executives may well provide the social life for such a resident. But for the Gringo who came to Baja to get away from everyday hassles, Tijuana is another big city with many of the problems faced in any other metropolitan area.

So, leaving the metropolitan area behind, the first place you might look is in *Las Playas* (the beaches) of Tijuana. This is close to the border — in fact one can walk across at low tide at the end of the fence where it meets the Pacific Ocean. It is a modern community, full of middle class and upper class Mexicans. Many of them live here and work in the United States, and there's a modern middle class suburban shopping mall rather than the usual tourist attractions.

There are high-rise condos on the ocean, and there are more than a few really spectacular mansions on the cliffs overlooking the ocean and on the hills overlooking the border fence. The latter locations have fabulous views of San Diego Harbor and Point Loma. In fact the hills around Las Playas probably have some of the most spectacular views in the entire world and they are largely undeveloped so far.

This is a Mexican community and probably no place for the Gringo who does not speak Spanish. If your taste is to share your life with other Americans, it is harder to do so in Las Playas than in some other parts of the coastal area. The distance to Tijuana and to the border is only ten or fifteen minutes, but the distance to Rosarito Beach where most of the Gringo activities take place takes the same or more time on the toll road. It is possible to get there by the free road, but that is almost 20 miles.

Just south of Las Playas is the first toll booth on the *cuota* or toll road to Ensenada; so residents must consider the cost of such tolls when searching in nearby *campos* or locations. First is Punta de Bandera, a beautiful spot on cliffs overlooking the Pacific, with a small beach under the cliffs. There are lovely homes here, many occupied by Gringos, and it surely rates as one of the more beautiful areas. One word of caution, however. The Tijuana sewage treatment plant is in the hills to the east of here, and sometimes, even passing on the toll road, one becomes aware of a distinctive odor. Luckily the prevailing breezes favor the Punta resident by blowing from the sea toward the east, considerably reducing that problem. There is easy on-and-off access to the highway in both directions from this location.

As far as smells are concerned, anyone who has visited much in any part of Mexico knows that the odor of burning trash or garbage is common in many places. Perhaps the dumps catch on fire accidentally; perhaps they are burned purposely, but for days or weeks the odor will hang in the air over a whole city. No Gringo is much affected, but if peculiar odors are a problem for you, maybe you shouldn't think too seriously of Mexico.

If you're still continuing with me on this tour of homesites, the next overpass to the south after Punta Bandera leads to a new development which promises marina, golf course, and many other amenities. Many millions of dollars in Mexican and U.S. money are rumored to be planned for investment there. At this writing, homesites are just going on sale, and condos are in the process of being built. If the future is not disappointing, this could be a great place.

Next south is the large colony of San Antonio del Mar, stretching over a mile along the sea on the right side of the toll road. Here the *cuota* skirts the side of the hills on the left, and the driver looks down to the right on the mostly white buildings with red roofs, lying against the azure sea. It would inspire almost any potential homeowner to stop right there to buy a home.

This is one of the longest established of the Gringo colonies, and it now has quite a few middle class Mexicans living there also. If one lives in the northern part of the colony, it is quite a trip along cobblestone streets to the entrance or exit on the southern end of the settlement, though it is hoped the new overpass just to the north may there connect San Antonio to the *cuota*. At present, at the southern end of the *campo* there is easy off- and-on access to the *cuota*, and one can drive all the way to south of Rosarito without paying a toll. But a toll is collected at Las Playas when going north.

As one continues south, there is constant development all the way to Rosarito. The northern colonies, Punta Blanca (brand new) and Baja Malibu also have easy on-and-off access to the toll road, but after that, residences to the west of the *cuota*, those on the shoreline, have access only to the south-bound lanes. It is necessary to travel about eight miles south to Rosarito in order to get across the toll road and head north again, not a disaster, surely, but something to be considered, especially since there are virtually no businesses available between there and the city of Rosarito.

A word of warning is also in order in regard to the condition of access roads to the homes in this and other areas. Sometimes roads are not properly maintained, and it is possible that during the rainy season, access in and out can be extremely difficult, even impossible. Bad rains don't happen very often in Baja, but they do occur from time to time.

Many of these homes along the coast all the way to Ensenada developed from the originally adventurous tourist who pulled a travel trailer down to the area and parked it on the beach or on one of the beautiful cliffs. Then the travelers began to discover that they came often; so they found a permanent place to rent, left the trailer and commuted on weekends. They built a permanent patio or porch, maybe enclosed it into another room. Finally they built walls around the trailer, added more porch or more rooms, etc., to create a lovely home with a beautiful view. Many such homes are still available for less than a down payment on a condo in the U.S., and some of them are in unbelievably beautiful sites! Unfortunately they are often in areas where roads, telephones, and other amenities have never reached to this day.

Whatever utilities are available in the older sites are seldom underground, and you should ask about the plans in the new facilities. Usually we Gringos are used to the sight of at least a power line slicing through our views of the ocean, maybe a power pole, and almost always TV antennae. But, after all, there's an awful lot of ocean to enjoy!

Rosarito proper is probably the heart of Gringo activities on the Azure Coast. It has long been the gathering place for denizens of the U.S. who in the 1920s wanted to enjoy gambling and night life, and since then have enjoyed the outdoor life, the tacos and beer of Baja. Now it is becoming the heart of the family resort vacation area, with accommodations ranging from the reasonably priced to the luxurious. The city now contains a population in the neighborhood of 100,000 people, with the prediction that it will double in the next decade. It is a genuine beach town, embodying both the good and the bad of that fate. Details on the benefits and caveats of settling in Rosarito will be found in the next chapter.

From there south, for some fifteen miles, there is one complex after another, providing all kinds of homes for all kinds of people. For the most part, the older places are somewhat less expensive, and there are *campos* where there is still some inexpensive housing, and some areas where the poor Mexicans can still find a place. But for mile after mile, there is recent or brand new construction. Check for the convenience of facilities available near the site you choose. Many new developments are promising to include shopping centers, but remember in Mexico that may be almost any decade from now. If driving at night is a problem, it may be that places close to Rosarito or farther down the coast near Ensenada are more practical choices.

After leaving La Mision, about fifteen miles south of Rosarito, the settlements thin out. The *cuota* runs along the coast on cliffs that discourage easy development, and the distances from both Rosarito and Ensenada still present problems. Rosarito is less than 30 minutes from the border, even without going on the *cuota*. But from there on south, the free road is definitely not easy driving, and the *cuota* does not have really frequent off-ramps. Therefore, the farther south, the more time it takes to get to the border or to any sizeable facilities.

Along this stretch, a little over 50 miles from the border, is the really large development called Bajamar. Here there is already a golf course, and other facilities are well developed. It's rumored that many millions more are going into marinas and other amenities, and a high-rise is going up. Rancho homesites are promised on the hills to the east of the *cuota*.

Another new development just south of there is El Mirador with, at this writing, a large recreation building completed and RV spaces available. This is the third luxury RV park between Tijuana and Ensenada. One is called El Oasis and is north of Rosarito on the *cuota*. About halfway to Ensenada from the border is the second one, La Yarda, and now El Mirador. These are truly luxury resorts with fine restaurants, swimming pools, satellite TV, and many other amenities. El Oasis even provides a shuttle bus to and from Rosarito.

Beyond El Mirador, the highway enters a geological fault zone, on which no homesites are planned. This is a surface fault, not deep or dangerous for major earthquakes, but it does subject the highway to frequent superficial damage, and houses would definitely slip away; in fact, just before entering Ensenada, some can be seen in various states of slippage on the hills above the *cuota*. Definitely not a place to make a permanent home!

Ensenada starts rather suddenly where the fault zone ends, and there is an additional chapter on the details of life there as they differ from the areas farther north. This too is a booming little city, very different from either Tijuana or Rosarito. It lies around a beautiful curved bay, and the Gringos live in a variety of places in this extensive area. The development of Gringo *campos* is not as evident as it has been in the trip down the coast; so familiarity with the area is definitely needed in order to make a good choice.

As you consider the hundreds of places you have seen, remember to take note of how you get to and from your dream home and how far you will have to go to get a bottle of milk or a loaf of bread. You might also check the construction, especially in the older houses. There was a time, not too long ago, when all cement was mixed by hand, and sometimes that could result in a house that seemed to be built of nothing but sand.

Don't forget to check on the utilities, especially telephones. If the complex is on a switchboard, talk to the neighbors to see if the service is satisfactory. Electricity is generally available almost anywhere, but it doesn't hurt to check.

Remember construction and sales laws are not as rigid as they are north of the border. For instance, there is no provision for termite inspection. That is not usually a serious problem as most homes are built on cement slabs or masonry foundations in Baja. Also, various complexes have rules about such things as how high one can build or positions for TV satellite dishes.

Look into the legal angles, and *then* examine the view. Don't let the beauty of the site carry you away unless you think that the vista will make any difficulties unimportant!

Before you finally decide, let's take a look at two relatively urbanized areas that are popular with Gringos — Rosarito and Ensenada. They both have unique characteristics that make them tempting to many people!

IS ROSARITO ONE'S HEAVEN ON EARTH?

A lot of Gringos think it is, but we're talking about a beach town, and there is much that is good and some bad involved.

The average tourist from the U.S. thinks of Rosarito as the five-mile-long stretch of wide, white sand that is the first major stretch of beach after Las Playas to the north. However, the actual area of Rosarito stretches from San Antonio Del Mar on the north to La Mision, some 35 miles south. You see, a municipality in Mexico is quite different from a city in the United States.

Until this past year, there were only four municipalities in the northern part of Baja California Norte: Mexicali in the east, Tecate in the mountains, Tijuana on the coast, and Ensenada, 70 miles south of there. Such municipalities are probably more like counties in the U.S. than they are like cities to us Gringos. For example, Tijuana has several *delegations*, or suburbs, each of which has its own governing council; one of these is Rosarito. The officials of the delegation are not elected by the voters, but rather appointed by the elected president of the municipality.

Now there are genuinely competing political parties in Baja, and delegation politics are becoming more important; so Rosarito, from San Antonio to La Mision, voted in September 1992 on becoming a separate municipality. The vote was overwhelmingly in favor, 7000 *si*, 400 *no*, but Mexican law requires a majority of the eligible voters to vote *si*, and the in-favor vote was 200 votes short. Everyone thought those 200 votes would be "found," but Mexican politics have certainly changed! the votes were not produced, and now there is an appeal before the state legislature. So-o-o-o, when you read this who knows whether or not Rosarito will be the fifth municipality in the area.

City or no, it's interesting to try to find out how many *Norte Americanos* live in the area. There are probably at least 5000 homes (some "authorities" estimate twice that number) owned under foreign *fideicomisos* or under mobile home leases. Some of these are weekenders' homes or belong to snow birds or desert dwellers who inhabit them only seasonally. The United Society of Baja California, the association of Gringos in the area, has grown to over 400 members. But nobody thinks that it represents anything like a majority of the full time, let alone seasonal, residents of the area.

Four years ago the opposition political party, PAN, took over in Baja Norte and in Tijuana, but even before that, changes began taking place in the infrastructure and development of Rosarito. All politicians in a competitive free government want to impress the voters with what they can do for them, and the former single party, the PRI, saw the handwriting on the wall before the '88 elections and started a program of improvement even before they went out of office.

Since that election the PAN party has been in power, and it appears to us outsiders that more public money is going into government services and infrastructure. Could that mean that less is disappearing into the pockets of the politicians?

With that summary on the superficialities of municipal politics in Mexico, we will now concentrate our thoughts and remarks on the approximately five-mile-long commercial stretch along the beach and the residential areas on either side of it.

The little city is showing enormous changes! There is now a working sewer system in Rosarito which is being gradually expanded. The dusty streets are gradually, very gradually, being surfaced, and chuck holes seem to be fewer, with repairs more timely than in the past. Police and firemen seem more professional, and their equipment is improving, in spite of the current warning by the U.S. Consulate that instances of exploitation of Gringos by the police is reappearing. If properly reported, the authorities make certain the offenders are removed from patrol or even from the force. Even compactor trash trucks are seen on the streets, and once recently there was a street sweeping machine raising and throwing much dust in every direction. Is that or is that not an improvement over the broom and shovel brigade who gather the dirt and shovel it into wheelbarrows? In any case, it does seem that facilities are constantly improving.

Such public improvements encourage private businesses and homes to also upgrade in many ways, and the town is gradually becoming cleaner and more attractive as time passes. The main boulevard, Benito Juarez, has been paved curb to curb and widened to four lanes of traffic, with access areas for buses and parking. New facades are appearing on its main street businesses, sidewalks are being installed or improved, and a new large shopping mall is under construction which is to be anchored by a fine Mexican department store. Nevertheless, it still behooves the pedestrian to watch for unexpected changes of level or unguarded holes in sidewalks. In Mexico, you always watch where you're walking!

Rosarito had and still has a long way to go. Many streets are impassable in hard rains, and the residents of the hillsides sometimes cannot even walk to bus stops because there are no sidewalks. Dust and sand build up quickly, and the soot from the electrical generating plant in the area is a constant source of black grit.

Some of the biggest problems occur on the beautiful beach. Under Mexican law, the beach is the responsibility of the federal government, and local police have no jurisdiction there. But the *Federales*, the federal law enforcers, are nowhere to be seen on the beach.

That means that horses stand in the sand, waiting to be rented by tourists, and that, when rented, they are ridden all over the beach, often carelessly or by inexperienced riders. They are a source of much contamination and of danger for those who sit on the sand. In recent years, three-wheelers have added to the noise, contamination and danger. Some of the bigger complexes and hotels have put steel posts on the upper part of the beach that keep the horses and three-wheelers from tearing through certain sections, and in some unexplainable way, the *vaqueros* who tether the lines of horses are convinced to keep a decent distance from such establishments' clean sand. Many hotels and other facilities hire people to clean and rake the beach in front of their properties, but there are no beach-cleaning machines like those that appear on U.S. beaches. There is no question but that the beach in general is neither a safe nor a pleasant place to be on a crowded weekend.

Another problem faced by the residents of Rosarito is the noise and vandalism engendered by some elements of the beach crowd who are out to have a "good time" at almost anyone's expense. Loud radios boom from auto stereo systems, and discos pump out dance music at an unbelievable volume. There are those who drink too much or indulge in drugs and who become noisy, rude, and sometimes even downright dangerous. Such people unfortunately are the curse of almost any beach town, but on Mexican beaches, only the federal soldiers are empowered to stop them, and there are no enforcers anywhere around.

And then there are the fireworks! 'Tis said that it's illegal to sell them, but the places that advertise them with big signs are innumerable. Most *campos*, with the fire danger in mind, ban them among the homes, but they are perfectly legal on the beach. In the early evening, they are not too distracting and are often pretty to watch, but throughout the night, those cherry bombs can certainly interrupt a good night's sleep.

The Spanish language newspaper in the area bemoans the problems on the beaches, and the citizens of Rosarito are shocked by some of the moral excesses that take place in public. Actually, the Mexicans have a very high sense of serious family values, and now that the government must be responsive if it hopes to remain in power, there is an expectation that such conduct will be curbed at least in some measure.

As the area becomes more developed, as buildings go up on formerly vacant lots where pickups full of young people used to congregate, as the police become more professional, and if Rosarito gains new power through municipal status, there is hope that the general aspect of the little city will be improved or at least confined to certain areas.

Given all of the described problems, the area still has great charms for the Gringos who think they might like to settle there. Many of the campos where Gringos settle are relatively isolated, especially outside the central area. When the holiday weekends are over, even the main part of the beach is once more inhabited primarily by the walkers, the joggers, and the surf fishermen. Hey! The winters are wonderful!

In the central area, residents can walk, if they so desire, to virtually any shop or service that is needed — banks, doctors, pharmacies, grocery stores, auto mechanics, city offices, etc. Or, if not in the mood for the walk, distances are short and uncomplicated by car. Parking, except on summer weekends, has not yet become a problem.

Beautiful homesites are still available in Rosarito at all price levels up to the ultimate luxury category and with all kinds of construction standards. New high-rises are built with cranes and steel beams, premixed concrete, and many prefabricated parts, even as they would be in the U.S. More and more architects and engineers are concerned about earthquake standards and incorporate such work into their plans, though laws in Baja are not as tough as in Southern California.

In some complexes, detail work is exemplary, and architectural planning represents the ultimate in beauty and comfort. Many are planned with full security, but the usual caveats still remain valid in regard to telephone service, water supply and other services. For instance: Who installed the elevators? Do they have service from Tijuana? How about smoke alarms? etc., etc. Take nothing for granted in Baja!

Rosarito has the proximity to the border that makes it ideal for those who plan to commute often. The trip is anything but onerous except for the actual border crossing, and that we Gringos learn to accept, or we don't become Baja Gringos. It also has the advantages of standards fast becoming, if not yet a part of the first world, at least far above the third world expectations.

Check your chosen location carefully for access, services, legal problems, nearby activities, the possibilities of storm damage, and in regard to other possible problems. But, if your prospective home-site can meet your requirements, there are many advantages to living in this particular somewhat urbanized corner of paradise. You are the one who will have to decide!

OR IS ENSENADA THE PLACE TO CHOOSE?

Its location, a little farther from the border, makes it more interesting for some people and less satisfactory for others. Herewith some information about the delights and the problems involved in living on this beautiful bay.

After passing through the final toll gate on the *cuota*, Ensenada really begins. This is no sleepy little fishing village as it once was. There is a drive of several miles through industrial areas on the left and tourist facilities on the right of the road, and finally the entrance road to the city takes the sightseer past some rather extensive shipyards before reaching the real tourist areas. This little city is on the only decent harbor on the Pacific in Northern Baja California, and therefore it has a considerable industrial base. More and more cruise ships are putting into port here, and tourism has always been an important part of its economy; so it's an interesting mix of tourism and industry.

The city lies around the beautifully curved bay, with hills rising all around it, and therefore has some perfectly beautiful homesites all over the area. Many Gringos have lovely homes up on the hills, but the majority still live in *campos* near the beach front. There is no beach in the center city area because the bay has been dredged to admit ships of deeper drafts, but south of the business district and clear around onto the peninsula that forms the southern side of the bay are many lovely Gringo colonies. Many also live on the hillsides with views that would be worth millions of dollars in the U.S. Most of the homes there are custom built, and the owners have what they consider a dream home in a corner of paradise. In fact, most would fit that definition for almost anyone.

From Ensenada proper, the drive to the border via the *cuota* is about an hour and a half, but it's much longer and more time consuming by the free road. In fact very few Gringos take that route. Because of the distance, Ensenada Gringos are more inclined to live more of their lives in Mexico rather than buzzing across the border for every little thing. Most of them have local doctors, and many of them go to local hospitals. There are at least two reportedly excellent ones, with standards very close to the best in the U.S. and with state-of-the-art equipment. One Gringa recently had a cat-scan there for

$300. Some Gringos have supplemental insurance for their Medicare that will cover the entire cost of illness in Ensenada, and many use the local facilities.

The town is much cleaner than the towns farther north, with wide paved streets that come as a great surprise to the tourists. Virtually the entire central section is paved and boasts good, working traffic signals. Even inexperienced Gringos find it easy to drive there. It is surprising to the average Gringo to see new housing tracts being built where the streets are already paved.

In fact the building in Ensenada is quite different than is seen on the more northern parts of the coast. In this town, the major construction seems to be middle class housing tracts where dozens of small to medium size homes are going up on neat city lots. There are virtually no high-rises, and Ensenadans say the few multi-storied buildings there were not built with cranes and ready-mix concrete. It's logical to assume that the heavy equipment is primarily in the border area, and the expense of transport down as far as Ensenada is not practical at present. Of course, anything coming from the other direction is even further away!

Utilities and services are plentiful and in good working order for the most part. Telephones are easier to get all the time, even as they are further north, and electricity usually stays off for only short times. They do ration water, however. Certain parts of town have no water for from four to six hours every day. The time varies from neighborhood to neighborhood, but not from day to day. So the residents are able to prepare for the dry spells. Most Gringos have U.S. post office boxes and either go north a couple of times a week to get their mail or rely on one of the mail shuttle services that are available to them. TV on the hills is often by antennae from Los Angeles and San Diego, but most Gringos have satellite dishes.

This city now numbers around 500,000 people, but as any Mexican will tell you at his first opportunity, Ensenada is the largest municipality in the world. It stretches well over 100 miles down the coastline and almost all the way across the peninsula to the east. Most of it is rural, with many excellent farming areas and particularly famous vineyards. By far the greatest number of the people live in the area around the bay, and the estimated 15,000 U.S. citizens almost all live somewhere near the water.

Ensenada has been the site of many potential industries from time to time in its history, usually founded by foreigners, English or German particularly. Most of them failed to materialize in the ways planned by their founders many years ago, but there are some that have lasted a good long time and are still there for the citizens and the tourists.

One is the famous Santo Tomas winery, the oldest in Baja California. The family has constantly improved the vintages, and it is hoped that it will soon be distributed in the U.S. Other fine wineries are developing there, among which the best liked at present is probably Cetto, also planning to go into the States with their product. However, beware. Baja wine is not cheap!

Of course, fishing has always been a big part of the city's economy, and it still is although the ban imposed by the U.S. on Mexican tuna because of their carelessness in killing dolphins has been very hard on the city. There is a fish cannery right in the heart of the city that cannot afford to move or expand because of the financial difficulties they face. This in spite of the fact that the fishermen now claim that they have corrected their nets and fishing methods. There is much unhappiness in this regard among the Mexican fishermen.

Sports fishing is usually great off the shore of Ensenada, and the commercial fishing boats bring in tons of beautiful fish virtually every day. There are fish markets along the waterfront, and Gringos soon come to expect to eat only fish that comes right off the boat.

Back in the '30s, just before the bubble of prosperity caused by gambling and legal alcohol burst in Baja, a beautiful hotel and casino was built on the beach of Ensenada. Jack Dempsey was one of the owners, and it was a place where the rich and famous played — but only for a very short time.

Repeal of prohibition in the States and the outlawing of gambling in Baja in the early '30s when the depression was at its worst, meant that the beautiful hotel closed its doors, and for many years it was a boarded up curiosity. Now it has been turned into a beautiful cultural center, where permanent and rotating art shows and museum exhibits are always available to the public. Various performances and concerts take place in its auditorium, and it is a beautiful place for important civic affairs. It adds much to the ambiance and cultural life of the city.

There is a spacious city park along the waterfront, and there are more and more attractive shopping complexes and delicious seafood restaurants going up in the area. They hide the shipyards that are along the north side of the bay, and they offer the tourist and town dwellers interesting places to eat and shop.

Maybe the most famous place in Ensenada from the standpoint of history and fun is Hussong's Bar. This has stood undisturbed for nearly a century now, with historical pictures on the walls and even sawdust on the floor. On crowded weekends it is almost impossible to find a place to sit or even stand. *Mariachis* get into the act, and there is even dancing on the table. The Hussongs are one of the oldest families in the area and descendants are in every aspect of life in Ensenada from fine arts to business.

Just beyond the central part of the city is a brand new eighteen-hole golf course, which my playing friends claim is really excellent. The Gringos complain that the charge for playing there is too high, and most golfers who live further north go across the border to play in the U.S.

There is an active social and service club for the Gringos, the Amigos of Ensenada, which boasts its own clubhouse. Such organizations are valuable, not only for the sociability provided, but also to keep the *Norte Americano* foreigners apprised of what is going on in the city and environs.

Real estate prices incline to be somewhat lower, perhaps, but there are virtually no new high-rise condos to compare with those farther north. In other ways, the prices vary as they do in other places on the location, construction, etc. Unless there is a magnificent house on it, $100,000 is considered an enormously high price for beach front property.

Public transportation is available from the one-day cruise ships that travel there from San Diego, and also by tourist bus from San Diego, both of which can provide for stays overnight or for several days. Mexicoach is also considering scheduled service from Tijuana for tourists who wish to visit there without their cars.

So Ensenada is a great place for the Gringos to congregate and to live. It's not quite as convenient for speedy border crossings as are the communities farther to the north, but it is one of the loveliest spots on the coast and urbanized enough to make life easy for the Gringos.

IS THERE LIFE BEYOND ENSENADA?

Depends on which way you're going! The south shore of Ensenada Bay is part of Baja that has long been a favorite of the Gringos, and it is seeing much current development. But south of there, life is more isolated and becomes quite different from Northern Baja.

The bay at Ensenada is really called Todos Santos, and its southern shoreline is a small, narrow peninsula called Punta Banda. The lee side of this peninsula is washed by a gentle surf, usually restrained by the curve of the bay. Parts of this area have been beloved by Gringos for many years, and parts of it are now undergoing luxurious development to attract tourists and residents from not only Canada and the U.S. but also from other parts of Mexico and the world.

From the end of the *cuota* north of Ensenada,

there is nothing resembling freeway driving. Ensenada has many four-lane boulevards, but they are bordered by businesses and have many stop lights. After dragging through the city, the first place of beauty and interest is Estero Beach, six miles out of the city. Since it's becoming increasingly less likely that the driver will know the city has been left behind, he or she must look for a sign for a right turn to Estero Beach, just past the military airfield (the only airfield in Ensenada).

It's only a few blocks down to the water, and the visitor finds himself in a beautifully landscaped compound which includes not only tourist-oriented facilities such as a fine hotel, good restaurant, shops, and even a lovely little pre-Columbian museum, but also a large mobile home park.

This place began in the late '30s as a fishing camp, and the present manager's grandfather used to provide bait and even take the Gringos out on fishing trips. The hotel and facilities sit on another little spit of land that creates a lovely protected inlet here where there is no surf and where water sports and bird life are both abundant. The vistas are of the mountains of Punta Banda and across the bay, the activity of the city of Ensenada. It's a delightful location, developed for both love and profit by a family who cherishes the place. Homesites there consist of only a limited number of mobile home spaces, though the beachfront areas around Estero Beach are fast becoming bedroom communities to

Ensenada.

Back on the main road, which at this point is going in a southeasterly direction, the driver continues on to the little settlement of Maneadora, and here the road forks. For the Gringo who chooses not to live too far from his native country, the right fork is the only practical one. That road goes along the shoreline of the bay on Punta Banda and ends at the really spectacular La Bufadora. The tip of the point has become a Mexican National Park to enhance the tourists' appreciation of the world's largest blow hole. None this writer has seen in other places can compare to the size and frequency of this natural phenomenon.

There are a few homesites on the point near the national park, but there are many others before one reaches the point. One of the most popular places for Gringos to live is in the colony of La Joya, which is seventeen miles from Ensenada. Here over 100 Gringos have homesites in revocable trusts from the owner who is most anxious to make them comfortable and happy. He has donated land for a clubhouse and other recreational activities, and the latest thing that the Gringos have built there is a beautiful little gem of a real, honest-to-goodness theater. This community is very active in all kinds of social and community activities, including a fine English language little theater group. The clubhouse, theater and other facilities have been built with donations of money from individuals, institutions, and local fund raising. The Gringos here certainly are an active and friendly group.

However, there are no telephones available. They all communicate happily with each other by CB radio. "Hello, Rusty Nail. This is Flying Penguin." Their water comes from a well on the property. Of course they buy propane as do all the other residents of Baja, and they have good and reliable electricity. Their north-facing beach provides them with good TV reception from, of all places, Los Angeles, and very few feel the need for satellite dishes.

They are more isolated than most Baja Gringos in that they have to cover the last dozen miles or so from the Maneadora turnoff on an unmarked, really inadequate two-lane road, maintained in places primarily by the owners along the route. Very few La Joya Gringos are willing to go any place where they must drive home after dark. It takes about two hours to get to the border where the border wait makes a trip into the U.S. and back an all-day proposition. Of course, they do as much as they can in Ensenada and go north only when they find it absolutely necessary.

They have a lovely place to live. Once again, a glorious beach with only the most gentle surf lapping against it. Behind them are the hills of Punta Banda, on which many have chosen to build fine homes, and in front of them the beauties of the bay and the lights of Ensenada.

Not quite as far out on the point is another sand

spit that branches off the road onto the bay. In this lovely spot is the truly elegant Baja Beach and Tennis Club. This is a membership-only facility, primarily for those who have chosen to build homes surrounding the luxury clubhouse. Up a sweeping circular drive lies the beautiful main building which is surrounded by delightful homes and condominiums. Two lovely restaurants, a cozy bar, a gorgeous swimming pool, exercise rooms, tennis courts and other facilities are here available to the membership. And next to the water protected by the sand spit is a beautiful boat house with all kinds of water sports facilities.

Once again satellite TV is not absolutely essential though it is available, and at the present time, there is a cellular telephone system for the use of the members. The lines of the Mexican telephone company have not yet arrived there either. Members are included in the Ensenada Country Club which is a relatively short way down the road toward town.

There are other smaller and less popular communities along this road from Maneadero all the way to Bufadora, but a large part of the area is a farming community at the foot of the mountains behind it. Virtually every inch is a beautiful drive.

Back in Maneadero, if the driver does not take the right fork to Punta Banda, he will be headed down Mexican Highway One which extends the length of the entire Baja peninsula. Once again the driver is on a two-lane road, poorly maintained, but certainly driveable. It even lacks the white line down the middle that most of us so much depend on. Nevertheless, eighteen-wheel truck and tractor rigs wheel along at breathtaking speed, carrying produce from further south to the markets of Tijuana and U.S. California.

It is 100 miles to the next settlement where Gringos have made homes in any numbers, San Quintin, and those numbers are very small. The drive is a beautiful one, with farming valleys reaching down to the sea and winding mountainous roads with wide vistas between each valley. But it is anything but a high speed road, which makes the distance long and tiring.

Someday there will be a *cuota* to the area, skirting Ensenada and making the mountains between the valleys more passable. When that day happens, San Quintin will be one of the favorite spots on the coast. It has two bays, one of which is almost totally enclosed with a big volcanic peninsula jutting into the middle of it. Already there are a few Gringo homes on that peninsula, though it is several miles off the highway over a road that is almost impassable. These people have to generate their own electricity, depend on water trucks to fill their individual reservoirs, and of course have no telephones. But you can be sure that everyone has satellite TV.

It's a potentially magnificent area, however, and most of the Gringos live in the more settled parts of the beach and town where they have telephones, etc. The San Quintin River runs all year, and if it were dammed and developed, this area could well become another Hawaii. Maybe someday there will be something other than dirt air strips for airplanes; maybe someday the highway will be developed; maybe someday they will dredge this almost landlocked harbor, and the yachts moored there will make it reminiscent of Newport Beach or San Diego. But this writer would be greatly surprised if such happened in her rather limited lifetime and certainly is not willing to invest there for the sake of children or grandchildren.

As the highway travels farther south, the Gringo communities become smaller and more isolated until one reaches the very tip at Cabo San Lucas where the tourist population and the fine airport make that part of the peninsula as accessible as any other part of Mexico. For those who love to live in isolated communities or even in communities that are popular with Gringos but are too far away to be convenient to Southern California, there are books devoted to such areas in Mexico, and they are available to any interested reader.

CONCLUSION

You've had a reader's tour of the Pacific Coast side of the northern part of the Baja California Peninsula. If you are still a potential Baja Gringo, you now have some idea of where you want to look for your particular spot to satisfy your particular life style. At the very least you know what to expect if you come to visit us.

If you like what you've read in this book, you may be one who will love living your life, either part time or full time, on the Azure Coast of Baja California. Life here has fewer guarantees and also fewer restrictions. The pace is slower, which certainly means it's less hectic. Things may not be quite as convenient, but they are certainly more beautiful. The atmosphere is somewhat foreign, but it's not far to more familiar turf. And, if in some places standards seem somewhat less than expected, costs are also somewhat less.

We Baja Gringos welcome your interest because it means you are our kind of person, willing to take a risk — ready and willing to enjoy life as much as possible while living it to the full in whatever way that means to you!

Hasta la vista! — until we meet!

INDEX

Agua Caliente Casino 10
Agua Caliente Racetrack 10, 52
Agua Caliente Spa 10
Airport
   Cabo San Lucas 193
   Ensenada military 188
   Tijuana 54
Ambulance 120
American Consul 65
   registration 76
Amigos de Ensenada 143, 186
Architectural planning 178
Art shows 150, 185
Azure Coast 14, 55

Bahia de los Angeles 12
Baja California 6, 7
   harbor 7
   history 7
   Norte 10
   Sur 10

Baja California, cont.
   Symphony 151
Baja Malibu 165
Baja Times vii, 4
Bajamar 167
Ballet 150
Bank expenses 107
Banking 107-109
Bar expenses 100
Baseball 145
Beaches 16, 17
   Rosarito 175-177
Beauty shops 118
   expenses 100
Binational Emergency Medical Care Committee 126
Border crossing 48, 69-71, 148, 178
Bribery 79, 81, 128
Broadway musicals 148
Bull ring 57
Business opportunities 109

Cabo San Lucas 12, 193

California gray whales
    13, 19
Car expenses 98
Car repair 99
Casa de Cultura 150
Central heating 16
Centro de Cultura 149
Chargers 148
Charity organizations
    143
Chula Vista 147
City park 185
Comforts 3
Construction
    blanco 137
    negro 137
Contractor 136-139
Costa Rica 2
Crime 78-84
    bribes 79, 81
    burglary 81
    murder 83
    rape 83
Criminal justice 30
Cruise ships 180, 186
Cultural center 185
Cuota (toll road) 57
Currency 104-111
    exchange rate 104

Dancers 150

Death 125
Dorian's department
    store 60
Driving 39-47
    gloriettas 51
    laws 42-45
    Mexican insurance
        45, 50
    road maintenance 41
    speed limit 57
    vehicle permits 42
Drug and alcohol
    sanitariums 56
Duty free stores 102

Earthquakes 22, 168,
    178
El Mirador 168
El Oasis 168
Electricity 85, 86
Employment 75
Ensenada 13, 14, 53,
    55, 61, 168, 180-186
    Bay 62
    Country Club 19
    distance to border
        181
Estero Beach 188
Exchange rate 105
Expenses 93-103
    bank 107

Expenses, cont.
  bar 100
  beauty shop 100
  car 98
  car repair 99
  duty free stores 102
  groceries 101
  handyman 94
  health care 94
  hotels 100
  housecleaners 94
  insurance 97
  liquor 101
  pharmaceuticals 94
  residential real estate 96
  restaurants 99
  skilled labor 95
  telephone 99
  utilities 99
  wardrobe 101

Fall 20
Federal District Attorney's Office for the Protection of the Consumer 133
Feminism 29
Fideicomisos 67, 129-132, 135, 172

Fiesta Americana Hotel 52
Fireworks 176
Fishing 184

Food
  safety 112, 114, 115
Free Trade Agreement 110

Gambling 9, 10
Gasoline 91
God and Mr. Gomez 140
Golf 13, 185
Green Angels 57
Gringos 152-160
  employees 152, 153
  full-timers 157
  part-timers 156
  population 11, 14, 172, 183
  retired 153
  weekenders 156
Groceries 101
Guadalupe Valley 61

Handyman 94
Harbor 180
Health and recreation centers 144

Health care 94
Health insurance 123
Holidays 28, 29, 145
Home building 135-140
   construction 137
   contractor 136
   Mexican architect 137
Hotel expenses 100
Housecleaners 94
Human rights 29, 30
Hussong's Bar 185

Imperial Beach 147
Income tax, U.S. 74
Indians 7, 8
Industrial polution 21
Insects 116
Insurance 45, 50, 97, 123
Investment 76

La Bufadora 62
La Joya 189
La Mision 17, 167
La Paz 12
La Yarda 168
Las Playas 57, 53, 55, 56, 162
Latino culture 23

Law 42-45
   alcohol 46, 64
   cigarettes 68
   customs 68
   liquor 68
   Mexican courts 67
   misunderstanding 80
   money 68
   motorcycle helmets 67
   Napoleonic Code 43, 45, 65
   pets 69
   seat belts 67
   tax return 67
   will 67
Libre (free road) 59
Liquor expenses 101
Loreto 12

Maja Beach and Tennis Club 191
Maneadora 189
Maquiladora 1, 151, 153
Medical care 3, 119
   ambulance 120
   diagnostic, laboratory 120
   emergency number 121
   health insurance 123

Medical care, cont.
  international
    cooperation 124
  Medicare 123
  Mexican dentists 120
  Mexican doctors 119
  pharmaceuticals 120
  Red Cross 121
  treatment 56
Medicare 123
Mexicali 12
Mexican
  architect 137
  Consulate 74
  dentists 120
  doctors 119
  folklorico 150
  government 11, 127
  Highway One 10, 191
  holidays 28, 29, 145
  insurance 45, 50
  National Park 189
  National Symphony 149
  Nationwide Association of Realtors 132
  people
    characteristics 23
  stock market 108
  theater 150
Mexicoach 186

Missions 9
Mobil home 96
Mulege 12
Museum 188
Musicians 150

National City 147
Newspapers
  Baja Times vii, 4
  Zeta 149
Noise 176

Odors 163
Opera 145
Otay Mesa 54
Outdoor activities 13, 142

Padres 148
Pageant of the Masters 148
Permits 3, 72-77
  investment 76
  renter's 73, 74
  resident visa 75
  tourist visa 72
  vehicle 41, 42
Peso 105
Pharmaceuticals 94, 120
Police 43, 44, 79-81, 174

Politics 30, 31, 32, 172, 173
Postal service 89
Prohibition 9, 10, 184
Propane 87, 88
Property ownership 127-134
Public restrooms 116
Punta Banda 62, 187, 189
Punta Blanca 165
Punta de Bandera 163
Rainfall 15, 17
Recreation 13
Red Cross 121, 143, 155
Religion 151
Renter's permit 73, 74
Rescue units
  Rescate Halcones (Rescue Hawks) 125
Resident visa 75
Residential real estate 96
Restaurants 99
  hygiene 113
Revolution of 1910 9
Roads
  access 165
  repair 40, 41, 173, 174

Rosarito 165, 166, 171-179
Rosarito Beach 4, 14, 53, 58, 60
Rosarito Beach Hotel 10, 61
Rosarito-Ensenada cuota 53
San Antonio del Mar 164, 171
San Diego 147
San Felipe 12
San Fernando shopping plaza 60
San Quintin 13, 62, 192
San Ysidro 68, 147
  border 49
Santa Ana 18
Sea of Cortez 7
Sewer 173
Shipyards 180
Shopping 50
Skilled labor 95
Social life 142-146
Social Security 2
Spaniards 8
Spanish language 33-38
State Attorney General for the Protection of Tourism 66, 133

Storms 19
  extreme 21
Summer 20
Superbowls 148
Swimming 117

Tax
  real estate 133
  return 67
  seller's 134
  U.S. income 74, 102
  value added 133
Telephone 88, 89, 99
Television 90
Temperatures 18, 19
Tides 16
Tijuana 12, 161
  airport 54
  Avenida Revolucion 50
  Caliente Racetrack 52
  Cultural Center 51
  driving through 48-54
  Fiesta Americana Hotel 52
  gloriettas 51
  Omnimax Theatre 51
  Paseo de los Heroes 52
  Plaza Amigo shopping complex 54
Time 25, 26

Todos Santos Bay 187
Tourism 180
Tourist visa 72
Transportation 46, 186

U.S.
  Border Patrol 56
  Consulate 11, 125, 126
  Customs 48, 49
  taxes 102
United Society of Baja California 136, 143, 172
Untidiness 26, 27, 182
Utilities 99, 110, 161, 166, 182
  bills 110
  electricity 85, 86
  propane 87, 88
  telephone 88, 89
  television 90
  water 86, 87

Vecinos de Punta Banda 143
Vehicle permits 42

Walking 145, 177
Wardrobe expenses 101

Water 86, 87
　rationing 182
　safety 112, 114
Weather 15
Wineries 61
　Cetto 184
　Santo Tomas 183
Winter 17

Zeta 149

Watch for these titles in the
Mature Reader Series

100 GOOD THINGS THAT HAPPEN AS YOU GROW OLDER
The best is yet to come! An uplifting gift book.
$8.95

THE REAL TRUTH ABOUT LIVING TRUSTS
Discover the trust that's right for you
$8.95

HOW TO FIND A JOB
When You're Over 50 — Don't Have a Resume — and Don't Know What to Look For!
$8.95

REMARRIAGE
In the Middle Years and Beyond
$8.95

If You're Over 50, YOU ARE THE TARGET
How to avoid getting ripped off
$8.95

TAKE A CAMEL TO LUNCH
and Other Adventures for Mature Travelers
$8.95

THE ENCYCLOPEDIA OF GRANDPARENTING
Hundreds of Ideas to Entertain Your Grandchildren
$8.95

DEALS AND DISCOUNTS
If You're 50 or Older
$8.95

I DARE YOU!
How to Stay Young Forever
$8.95

**START YOUR OWN BUSINESS
AFTER 50 – OR 60 – OR 70!**
64 People Who Did It Tell You How
$8.95

THE BEGINNER'S ANCESTOR RESEARCH KIT
For the Beginning Genealogist
$7.95

OVER 50 AND STILL COOKING!
Recipes for Good Health and Long Life
$8.95

Write or call for our free catalog.
Bristol Publishing Enterprises, Inc.
P.O. Box 1737
San Leandro, CA 94577
(800) 346-4889 — in California (510) 895-4461